On Thursday, 22 June 1944, on the third anniversary of the German Army's invasion of the Soviet Union, the Red Army launched a series of massive offensives, codenamed Operation Bagration, aimed primarily at the sector of the front held by the divisions of Generalfeldmarschall Ernst Busch's Heeresgruppe Mitte between Vitebsk and Kiev in what is today Belarus and northern Ukraine. Although the Germans had managed to stabilise the front line during the winter and spring, their units had been badly depleted by the battles of the previous year and Busch's army group could muster less than 600 tanks and assault guns. In addition some of the best armoured units had been transferred to the west where the defensive battles in Normandy, although largely successful up to that point, were proving a constant drain on the army's resources. To make matters worse, the Germans had in fact anticipated that any large-scale Russian assault would come much further to the south against the divisions of Heeresgruppe Nordukraine, believing that the enemy would strike towards Warsaw and the Vistula, and to counter the expected threat the entire operational reserve for the Eastern Front had been sent to the southern sector.

When Operation Bagration commenced, the men of Heeresgruppe Mitte were opposed by 4,000 Soviet armoured vehicles and by the end of the month the better part of three German armies had been destroyed and Russian spearheads had penetrated deep into the German rear.

On 2 July, during a briefing held forward headquarters at Rasten East Prussia to discuss the si Hitler suggested that the ad Russian formations that were thre to encircle the entire army group could be cut off and eliminated by formally organised Kampfgruppen, or battle groups (1).

To the complete surprise of the officers present, the Führer proceeded to give a detailed explanation regarding the organisation, weapons and equipment of the proposed Kampfgruppen, maintaining they be called brigades and that each should be made up of an armoured infantry battalion, a tank battalion of approximately thirty to forty vehicles, a company of towed anti-tank guns and a number of mobile anti-aircraft weapons. It soon became obvious that this was something more than an off-the-cuff remark when Hitler went on to state that a total of twelve brigades would be required and as they would be expected to operate into the winter months, it would be essential that the Jagdpanzer 38(t) Hetzer tank destroyer, which was almost ready to enter service, be fitted with wider tracks (2).

As early as the following day the Organizations-Abteilung of the army high command had prepared a proposal suggesting that the Panzer divisions that were at that time being rebuilt be converted to what was referred to as Panzer-Kampfgruppen. The first five would contain an armoured battalion equipped

from badly depleted infantry formations supported by a few tanks and artillery pieces.

2. Interestingly, this idea resurfaced in January 1945 with the formation of Panzer-Jagd-Brigade 104 which was equipped with StuG IV assault guns and Hetzer tank destroyers but lacked an infantry element.

A Panther ausf G of Panzer-Regiment 16 photographed in the town of Bures just prior to the counterattack at Lunéville. Note the pattern of Zimmerit application typical of MAN-assembled tanks, the welded exhaust guards and the sheet metal covers of the exhaust mufflers which were incorporated into production from June 1944.

A Panther ausf G of 2.Kompanie, Panzer-Abteilung 107 photographed near Overloon in Holland some time after the war. This tank is also shown on page 23 of the Camouflage & Markings section.

anti-tank company. The remaining seven Panzer-Kampfgruppen would be outfitted with either Pzkpfw IV tanks or Panthers as they became available. This idea was rejected out of hand by the Führer and on Friday, 7 July 1944 a revised table of organisation developed by the Inspekteur der Panzertruppen, which was essentially based on Hitler's original directions, was submitted. This was eventually accepted and an order issued on the following Tuesday calling for the formation of ten brigades to be numbered from 101 to 110.

It was anticipated that the brigades numbered 101 to 104 would be ready for combat by 15 August 1944, while those numbered 105 and 106 would be operational by the end of the same month, with Panzer-Brigaden 107 and 108 ready by the middle of September and two weeks after that Panzer-Brigaden 109 and 110 would leave for the front. The original order was amended on 24 July 1944 and official tables of organisation were issued but little changed other than to grant the honour title Feldherrnhalle to Panzer-Brigade 106 and Panzer-Brigade 110. On 6 August 1944 new orders were issued directing that the brigades numbered 105 to 110 were to receive additional support units but in reality all the Panzer brigades were understrength to some extent and not all the official instructions were implemented.

Why Hitler accepted the reduction in the number of brigades from twelve to ten is still something of a mystery but during a meeting to discuss the Westwall defences held on 1 September 1944, Generalmajor Wolfgang Thomale, Guderian's chief of staff, suggested that three Panther battalions that were at that time being formed in Germany be used to create what he called 'mobile Panzer brigades'. And so Panzer-Brigaden 111 to 113 were ordered into existence. The organisation of these new formations was significantly different to the earlier units and although most accounts usually mention two types of establishment I have chosen to divide the brigades into three categories or generations and the reason for this is explained in the main text and the accompanying charts.

Brief histories of the Panzer brigades and tables of organisation are contained in the following pages but it should be remembered that these units were rushed into service and existed for a short period of time. While our knowledge of certain brigades could fairly be described as comprehensive, information on others is almost non-existent and where I have been forced to resort to speculation I have tried to make this clear. Although some aspects have already been mentioned in *Panther Tanks: German Army and Waffen-SS Normandy Campaign 1944* and *Panther Tanks: German Army and Waffen-SS Defence of the West 1945,* the third and eighteenth books respectively in this series, I have included them here to give the reader a more complete picture of the organisation of these formations and the weapons with which they were equipped.

THE FIRST GENERATION PANZER-BRIGADEN 101-104

The formation of the Panzer brigades was so rushed that in most cases our knowledge of the actual organisation is limited to the few surviving documents and combat reports. Panzer-Brigaden 101-104 completed their training at approximately the same time and their establishments were essentially identical. The Panzergrenadier and Pionier elements are examined in more detail in the charts for the second and third generation brigades..

Stab Panzer-Kampfgruppe

This title was in use at least until 7 July 1944 and possibly longer. The Brigade-Stab was made up using parts of KstN 1104a (gp) von 1.4.1944 Stab und Stabskompanie eines Panzergrenadier-Regiments a (gp). The initial 7 July 1944 proposals give two Sdkfz 251/3 halftracks.

Stabskompanie	Gruppe Führer	

Nachrichten-Zug	Erkunder-Zug	Aufklärung-Zug	Panzer-Werkstatt-Kompanie	Grosse Kraftwagenkolonne (60t) KstN 1231 von 1.11.1943

The Stabskompanie was based around the Gruppe Führer components of the Aufklärung-Zug from KstN 1107 (fG) von 1.4.1944 Stab und Stabs-Kompanie einer Panzer-Abeilung (frei Gliederung) or possibly KstN 1107a(fG) von 1.4.1944, both listed as preliminary amendments and superseded in the following November. This unit contained the Gruppe Führer with two Sdkfz 251/18 Beochtungspanzerwagen halftracks, although the exact type is unknown, and one Sdkfz 251/1 halftrack. The Stabskompanie also included Truppen 1-4 of the Erkunder-Zug from KstN 1150 (fG) von 1.4.1944 Stabskompanie Panzer-Abteilung (frei Gliederung) and was probably made up of the Gruppe Führer with one halftrack, one VW light car and one Kettenkrad. The Truppen had four halftracks and one Kettenkrad. This was a light scouting unit and was not expected to engage the enemy as the Aufklärungs units were. It is likely that very few, if any, of the Panzer brigades received their allocations of Kettenkrad motorcycle-halftracks. In addition to the Erkunder-Zug, Sanitatsstaffel and Gefechstross units were also included in the 7 July 1944 recommendations but were not formally organised with various KstN until the compilation of the 18 July proposal. As the repair and maintenance units of the Panzer and Panzergrenadier battalions were for the most part never formed, the Panzer-Werkstatt-Kompanie undertook all the brigade's mechanical repairs. It was based on KstN 1187(fG) von 1.4.1944 Panzerwerkstattkompanie eines Panzerregiments (frei Gliederung) Pz.Abt Panther und Pz.Abt IV.

Stab Panzer-Abteilung (fG) KstN X von 15.7.1944	

Panzerbefehlswagen V   *Pzkpfw V*   *Pzkpfw V*

Fliegerabwehr-Zug		Panzer-Werkstatt-Zug

FlakPz IV 3.7cm   *FlakPz IV 3.7cm*   *FlakPz IV 3.7cm*   *FlakPz IV 3.7cm*

The battalion headquarters was formed using KstN 1107a (fG) von 1.4.1944 Stab einer Panzerabteilung (frei Gliederung) with parts of KstN 1150 (fG) von 1.4.1944 Stabskompanie einer Panzer-Abteilung (frei Gliederung), but without the five tanks of the Aufklärungs Zug normally included in the latter. Attached was a self-propelled anti-aircraft unit based on KstN 1196 (fG) v 1.9.1944 Teileinheit Panzer-Fliegerabwehr-Zug 3.7cm (frei Gliederung) made up of two Gruppen each with two 3.7cm Panzer-Flak guns. The original order, Nr.I/18056/44, also mentioned two fully-tracked 2cm anti-aircraft guns but I have been unable to find any mention of these in any other sources. The Panzer-Werkstatt-Zug, which would normally have been controlled by the Stabskompanie, was never formed. Note that in some brigades all three tanks of the Abteilung Stab were Panzerbefehlswagen V command tanks.

Panzer-Kompanie KstN XI von 15.7.1944	Panzer-Kompanie KstN XI von 15.7.1944	Panzer-Kompanie KstN XI von 15.7.1944	Panzer-Kompanie (Panzerjäger)

11 x Pzkpfw V	11 x Pzkpfw V	11 x Pzkpfw V	11 x Jagdpanzer IV

The Panzer company organisation was based on KstN 1177 (fG) von 1.4.1944 Panzer-Kompanie 'Panther' (frei Gliederung) with two Pzkpfw V Panther for the Gruppe Führer, or company commander, but with three platoons made up of three tanks each and not the normal allocation of five. KstN XI was officially replaced by KstN 1177 (fG) on 26 July 1944 but there was no significant change and the authorised number of tanks remained at thirty-six. The Gruppe Führer also had two light cars but most companies did not receive their two authorised Kettenkrad motorcycle-halftracks. The additional 4.Kompanie was based on KstN 1149 (fG) von 1.4.1944 Panzerjäger (Sturmgeschütz) Kompanie (frei Gliederung) and also amended to contain eleven vehicles. It is possible that an unnumbered KStN, dated 15.7.1944 and very similar to KstN 1149 (fG), may have been used for the early brigades as it authorised only eleven Jagdpanzer IV tank destroyers instead of the fourteen allocated by KstN 1149. In any event, none of the first generation brigades received their allocation of tank destroyers and shortly after Panzer-Brigade 104 left for the front the fourth company was dropped from the table of organisation.

Panzergrenadier-Bataillon

Panzergrenadier-Kompanie	Panzergrenadier-Kompanie	Panzergrenadier-Kompanie	Pionier-Kompanie

The Panzer-Pionier-Kompanie was attached directly to the Panzergrenadier battalion until the revisions of 18 July 1944 when it was subordinated to the brigade headquarters. Each brigade's major component units were identified by a number arrived at by adding 2000 to the brigade's number. For example, Panzer-Abteilung 2101, Panzergrenadier-Bataillon 2101 and Panzer-Pionier-Kompanie 2101 were all attached to Panzer-Brigade 101. Brief histories of the first generation brigades are given on the following pages.

Notes

1. Panzer-Ersatz-Abteilung 5, stationed at Neuruppin, north-west of Berlin, was responsible for the supply of replacements for Panzer-Brigade 101.

2. Oberst Schmidtgen was killed on 25 August 1944 near Puhja in Estonia, on a day when the brigade reported the loss of a single Panther, and replaced by Oberstleutnant Guido von Wartenberg.

3. Strachwitz's battle group was subsequently renamed as Panzer-Verband von Lauchert although it is referred to in some official documents as Panzer-Division von Lauchert.

Panzer-Brigade 101. Formed at the Mielau and Arys training grounds in East Prussia on 21 July 1944, the brigade was to be built around the remnants of 18.Panzergrenadier-Division but as that formation had been almost completely destroyed during the summer battles on the Eastern Front, the first units were created from Panzer-Brigade 10, a training unit, and Panzerjäger-Regiment 656. The brigade's Panzer-Abteilung 2101, which had been raised from elements of Panzer (Flam.) Abteilung 102 'Neuruppin' (1) and parts of 18.Panzer-Division, consisted of three companies of Panther tanks and a fourth company which was to be equipped with Pz IV/70 tank destroyers.

The first allocation of nine tanks was made on 13 July 1944, although it is unclear when these arrived. These tanks were all Panther ausf G models and in addition, two Bergepanther recovery tanks were also shipped to the brigade in place of the authorised Bergepanzer III.

By 1 August, a further twenty-seven Panthers had been despatched from the Heereszeugamt, giving a total of three tanks for the battalion headquarters and eleven for each of the three tank companies. The allocation of eleven Jagdpanzers for the Panzer battalion's 4.Kompanie never materialised and it seems that the crews remained at Mielau until they were dispersed to other units including schwere Panzerjäger-Abteilung 655 and Panzer-Brigade 150.

The brigade's commander, Oberst Meinrad von Lauchert, and his staff left for the Eastern Front in early August 1944 and were attached to Panzer-Verband von Strachwitz which was involved in the defensive battles in Latvia. The bulk of the brigade arrived in the East in mid-August but it is likely that Lauchert remained with the headquarters of Strachwitz's battle group and the command of Panzer-Brigade 101 passed to Oberst Richard Schmidtgen (2). The brigade took part in the fighting to restore a link with 16.Armee of Heeresgruppe Nord at Tukkum on the Gulf of Riga, supported by the Waffen-SS units of Kampfgruppe Gross and the guns of the heavy cruiser *Prinz Eugen*, entering the town during the afternoon of 21 August 1944.

On the following day the commander of Panzer-Abteilung 2101, Major Friedrich-Wilhelm Breidenbach, was seriously wounded and just two days later Generalmajor Graf von Strachwitz was badly injured in an automobile accident leaving command of the Kampfgruppe to Lauchert (3).

Said to have photographed near Elva in southern Estonia, in September 1944, the Panther ausf A shown above and the Panther ausf G at right are both from Panzer-Abteilung 2101. At the time Panzer-Brigade 101, with SS-Panzer-Brigade Gross, formed part of Panzer-Verband von Strachwitz. These images are taken from a series which shows that several of the battalion's tanks seem to have been marked with a black panther design on the turret side and a possible interpretation of this is shown in the Camouflage & Markings section. The placement of the Balkenkreuz on the hull side of the Panther ausf G would suggest that this is a Daimler-Benz production vehicle and the camouflage may be an early version on one of the factory-applied schemes.

With the capture of Riga, Panzer-Brigade 101 was moved by rail to Elva, south-west of Tartu in Estonia, and placed under the command of Armee-Abteilung Narva. Here the tanks of Panzer-Abteilung 2101 were involved in a series of successful counterattacks around Lake Wirz, modern-day Vortsjärv, but by early September, as the Germans withdrew from Estonia, the brigade returned to the area around Riga which was once again under threat. For the remainder of the month Panzer-Brigade 101 was engaged in series of defensive actions south-west of Riga around the villages of Bauske and Kacava near the present-day Lithuanian border.

In the first week of October 1944 the brigade supported 5.Panzer-Division in an attack near the village of Kraziai, west of the road between Siauliai and Kelme in northern Lithuania but ran into strong opposition and by the end of the day the Russians had been able to open an 8 kilometre wide gap between the two armoured formations. That night the Soviets managed to overrun the positions of 548.Grenadier-Division, which held a large section of the front, and on the following day pushed a strong mechanised force into the resulting breach. By noon on Saturday, 7 October 1944, the tanks of 5.Panzer-Division had been forced back to Stulgiai, on the Memel to Kaunas road, and Panzer-Brigade 101 was engaged in a fighting withdrawal near Kvedarna, a further 40 kilometres to the west.

The German formations managed to withdraw into the prepared defences of the Ostpreussen Line and on 19 October 1944 ten new Panthers were delivered to the brigade from Nachschub Ost (1). Within days, the tanks of Panzer-Brigade 101, subordinated to Fallschirm-Panzerkorps Hermann Göring, took part in the successful counterattack to retake Nemmersdorf, today Mayakovskoye in Russia, and in early November the brigade was involved in the recapture of Goldap, near the Polish border.

After the fighting for Goldap was concluded the remnants of the brigade were withdrawn from the front and transferred to the training facility at Arys in East Prussia where, on 16 November 1944, Panzer-Brigade 101 was formally disbanded. Most of the personnel of Panzer-Abteilung 2101 were used to form the second battalion of Panzer-Regiment 21 which was commanded by Major Breidenbach who had returned to the front after being wounded as mentioned earlier.

Panzer-Brigade 102. The brigade was formed on 20 July 1944 from elements of Reserve-Panzer-Division 233 and 25.Panzer-Division and commanded by Major Curt Ehle, a veteran of the Afrikakorps (2). The brigade was to be ready to move to the front on 15 August and by the end of July 1944 a total of thirty-six Panther tanks had been received by Panzer-Abteilung 2102 with an additional two Begepanther recovery tanks allocated to the Panzer-Werkstatt-Zug in place of the authorised Bergepanzer III. Although the last twenty-eight tanks received were almost certainly all Panther ausf G models, photographic evidence suggests that the first delivery, which was dispatched by the Heereszeugamt on 16 July 1944, contained at least some earlier models. The authorised Jagdpanzers of the battalion's fourth company were never delivered and the men remained in Germany and later incorporated into the Panzerjäger battalion of 13.Panzer-Division.

In mid-August the brigade was transferred to the Eastern Front and was involved in a series of counterattacks between the Bug and Narew Rivers in eastern Poland, notably between Ostroleka and Lomza where the tanks were able to prevent a Russian breakthrough aimed at the Vistula River crossings north-west of Warsaw.

On 8 September 1944 the battalion reported that, from an authorised total of thirty-six tanks, just thirteen Panthers were combat ready while a further three were in short-term repair (3). It seems that until early October the available tanks were formed into two understrength companies. During September the brigade was again in action at the Narew bridgehead, this time driving the Russians back across the river.

In early October 1944 the brigade was assigned to 2.Armee as an operational reserve and at that time reported that the number of tanks available for immediate deployment had risen to twenty-two and the Panthers were again formed into three companies. This increase was probably due to the return of vehicles which had been in long-term repair as the brigade's workshops were inadequate and based far behind the front line, a fact of which Major Ehle and the commander of XXIII.Armeekorps, General Otto Tiemann, complained on several occasions. In any case there is no official record of any allocation of new tanks.

On 11 October 1944 the brigade was subordinated to 25.Panzer-Division and took part in the defence of the area between Mlawa and Neidenburg, today Nidzica in northern Poland, fighting for the first time on German territory. In the brief but savage battles here up to ten Soviet assaults were repulsed and Oberfeldwebel August Burgholte, a platoon commander of the battalion's 3.Kompanie, was later

............continued on page 7

Notes

1. Nachschub Ost was the Army's supply directorate for all units serving on the Eastern Front.

2. Ehle's promotion to Oberstleutnant was not made until 1 November 1944.

3. Accounts which give a total of thirty-eight are probably including the two Bergepanther recovery tanks. Although no official figures are available it is unlikely that the battalion lost twenty tanks in the August battles, given that personnel casualties were relatively light, and a number of these vehicles may have been in long-term repair.

A Panther ausf A of Panzer-Brigade 102 photographed during the fighting in the Baltic States in September 1944. Although heavily camouflaged the turret number, which appears to begin with a 2, is just visible. This tank is also featured in the Camouflage & Markings section on page 17.

............continued from page 5

awarded the Ritterkreuz in recognition of his bravery and leadership, the only soldier of the brigade to receive the medal. Within two days the front had been stabilised and the brigade was transferred back to the defensive line along the Narew River, this time supporting 7.Infanterie-Division.

On 17 October the brigade was transferred to area between Gumbinnen and Treuburg in East Prussia, near the Lithuanian frontier, and driving straight from the rail yards to the front line, supported an attack attacked on the Red Army positions around the town of Goldap (1).

Placed under the command of 561.Volksgrenadier-Division, the tanks of Panzer-Brigade 102 was at first able to contain the Russians and then throw them back by the end of the month. But the heavy fighting had taken its toll and on 31 October 1944 Panzer-Abteilung 2102 reported that just twelve Panthers were combat ready with five in short-term repair. Many of the tank crews had been fighting as infantry for some time.

During the first week of November the brigade was moved to Kolno, north of Lomza in what is today eastern Poland, and fought for two weeks in the thick forests around the town in support of men of 28.Jäger-Division.

On 27 November 1944, after almost four months of continuous front-line service, Panzer-Brigade 102 was formally dissolved and a total of seventeen Panthers, including two Befehlspanzers, were handed over to 7.Panzer-Division, as were most of the brigade's remaining personnel and equipment. Major Ehle was promoted, as mentioned earlier, and awarded the Oak Leaves to his Ritterkreuz for his actions during the fighting in East Prussia.

Panzer-Brigade 103. Formed on 21 July 1944, the brigade's Panzer-Abteilung 2103 was created by renaming Panzer-Abteilung Norwegen which had been raised from the first battalion of Panzer-Regiment 9.

The first eight Panthers were allocated to Panzer-Abteilung 2103 from the Heereszeugamt on 25 July and by 1 August 1944, a further twenty-eight had been issued, making a full complement of thirty-six. These tanks were all Panther ausf G models. A planned fourth company never received their allocation of Jagdpanzer tank destroyers and the crews were eventually absorbed by 10.Panzergrenadier-Division.

In mid-August Panzer-Brigade 103 was transferred from Grafenwöhr in Germany to Truppenübungsplatz Arys in East Prussia but before the brigade's training could be completed Oberst Treuhaupt, the commander, was ordered to move his tanks to the front (2). In the area around Tukkum on the Gulf of Riga the Panther battalion's tanks supported Panzer-Verband von Strachwitz in a week-long assault to break through the Soviet lines to the encircled units of 16.Armee in Riga. After the town was retaken the brigade was withdrawn and held as an operational reserve for 4.Armee. At that time the Panzer battalion reported that thirty-three Panthers were on hand from an authorised strength of thirty-six. As the report does not list any tanks as being in repair it is assumed that three vehicles were completely destroyed in the battles in Latvia.

In September 1944 the brigade was transferred to East Prussia, taking part in the fighting around Gumbinnen and Schlossberg, halting a major Soviet advance in front of the village of Ebenrode, modern-day Nesterov in Russia. By the end of October the brigade was again transferred to the command of 4.Armee but the recent fighting had taken its toll and the Panzer battalion could only muster fifteen serviceable tanks, while another eight were in repair.

Beginning on Thursday, 9 November 1944 the brigade staff, with the surviving tank crews of Panzer-Abteilung 2103 and the maintenance platoon, were moved to Bielefeld in western Germany and the remaining Panthers and Bergepanther recovery vehicles (3) were handed over to Panzer-Regiment 21.

The brigade staff remained together for some time serving on the Western Front as the headquarters of Kampfgruppe Führer-Begleit-Brigade. From 20 January 1945 the staff, now commanded by Oberst Werner Mummert, was used to build the regimental headquarters of Panzer-Regiment z.b.V. Coburg (4) which was made up of the first battalions of Panzer-Regiment 29 and Panzer-Regiment 39 and the second battalion of Panzer-Regiment 9.

In some accounts Panzer-Regiment z.b.V. Coburg is referred to, somewhat confusingly, as Kampfgruppe Panzer-Brigade 103 and although a number of the brigade's personnel were certainly present, it should not be considered a reformed or resurrected version of the original formation.

Commanded by Oberstleutnant Kuno von Meyer, Panzer-Regiment z.b.V. Coburg fought in the Oder bridgehead battles of February 1945 and in March the Panzer-Brigade 103 staff were absorbed by Panzer-Division Müncheberg.

Notes

1. Gumbinnen was renamed Gusev in 1945 and Trueberg is today known as Olecko. Goldap must be one of the very few East Prussian place names that that was not changed by the Soviets.

2. Although this officer is usually identified as Kurt Treuhaupt, who later became the last commander of 16.Panzer-Division, I have been unable to confirm this. In any case he was replaced in November 1944 by Oberst Mummert.

3. Two Bergepanthers had been allocated to Panzer-Abteilung 2103 in late July 1944 in place of the planned Bergepanzer III vehicles.

4. The term zur besonderen Verwendung (z.b.V) can be translated as 'for special purpose' and is often encountered in references to ad-hoc formations.

A Bergepanther recovery tank based on the Panther ausf G hull. Note the raised superstructure at the centre of the hull and the spade, just visible at the hull rear, in the raised position. Note also the two large reinforced bumpers at the hull front. This is one of the vehicles of schwere Panzerjäger-Abteilung 512 which surrendered to the Americans at the town of Iserlohn in western Germany on 16 April 1945.

The Bergepanther was a turretless version of the Panther tank used for vehicle recovery under fire. They were issued, when available, to the Werkstatt companies of Panther, Tiger and Jagdpanther battalions. The first Bergepanthers were employed during Operation Zitadelle in June 1943 and these were based on Panther ausf D hulls. These early recovery tanks were a hastily designed and manufactured expedient and it was not until September 1943 that a purpose-built hull, based on the Panther ausf A, was available. The final configuration featured a rectangular opening in the hull top with a raised superstructure, a 40-ton winch and a large spade which was attached to the rear hull. Problems with the supply of parts for both the winches and spades were never adequately solved and it is known that many vehicles were delivered without either. Nevertheless, the scarcity of photographs depicting Bergepanthers without these items would suggest that both were retro-fitted. The design included provision for a 2cm Kampfwagenkanone 30 L/55 gun, mounted on the hull front, and while the hulls of the first few Panther ausf G versions were drilled to accept the gun mount there is no evidence that the guns were ever fitted. The firms of Maschinenfabrik Augsburg-Nürnberg AG (MAN), Daimler-Benz and Henschel produced Bergepanthers, although the latter were in fact based on MAN-manufactured hulls, until March 1944 when DEMAG assumed sole production. A total of 217 vehicles had left the Demag assembly lines by February 1945 and it is quite possible that a number were produced in March but reliable records are not available for the last weeks of the war. A further sixty-one Bergepanthers were converted from damaged Panther ausf D hulls by the firm of Siebert between August 1944 and March 1945. These vehicles were equipped with an unditching beam and the 2-ton Behelfskran but were not fitted with winches or spades and were in fact intended as support vehicles for the recovery tanks already in service. As the first deliveries of Bergepanthers based on the Panther ausf G chassis commenced in October 1944 it seems likely that the vehicles allocated to the Panzer brigades, at least the first generation units, were built on Panther ausf A hulls.

Notes

1. This formation was a division in name only and provided trained personnel for tank and motorised infantry units. It was stationed in Denmark.

2. Gehrke later gave evidence at the trial of the conspirators as the representative of OKW.

3. Another six tanks were despatched from Nachschub Ost on 27 August after the battalion had arrived in the East.

Panzer-Brigade 104. The brigade was formed on 18 July at Fallingbostel in Germany from various training units and parts of 233.Reserve-Panzer-Division (1).

Command of the brigade was given to Oberstleutnant Kurt Gehrke, an infantry officer who almost certainly owed his appointment to his part in thwarting the July Plot against Hitler's life (2). The brigade's armoured battalion, Panzer-Abteilung 2104, commanded by Major Wilhelm Weidenbrück ,was organised with three tank companies equipped with Pzkpfw V Panther ausf G tanks. A planned fourth company never received its Pz IV/70 tank destroyers and the crews were eventually assigned as reinforcements to the second company of Panzerjäger-Abteilung Grossdeutschland. The first allocation of tanks was made on 26 July 1944 and by 3 August the full complement of thirty-six had been issued and these were probably all Panther ausf G models (3). Before the brigade's training could be completed orders were received to move to East Prussia and the first elements arrived in the town of Eydtkau, modern-day Chernyshevskoye, on 16 August 1944 and within two days the last vehicles had been unloaded.

From 21 August the brigade's tanks took part in a series of counterattacks along the Lithuanian border near Schaken in support of the 561.Volks-Grenadier-Division and 1.Infanterie-Division and by the end of the month had been assigned to 2.Armee as an operational reserve. On 1 September 1944 the brigade reported that from a total authorised strength of thirty-six Panthers, just fourteen were combat-ready while three were in repair. This total includes the six tanks that were despatched from Nachschub Ost on 27 August 1944. For most of September the brigade was engaged in defensive actions at the Narew River bridgehead supporting the Grenadiers of 292.Infanterie-Division and 542.Volksgrenadier-Division. The fighting here was quite intense and by the end of the month the tank strength of Panzer-Abteilung 2104 had been reduced to nineteen serviceable Panthers with four in repair. On Tuesday, 24 October the tanks of the brigade supported an attack made by 62.Infantrie-Division between Swelice and Klepowo, west of Rozan in central Poland and on the following Thursday, despite heavy losses, the brigade was again thrown into battle in an attempt to relieve an infantry formation encircled at Pulutsk, further to the south. The Panthers were then rushed back to Klepowo were the situation had become so desperate that the brigade staff fought in the front line. It was here that Oberstleutnant Gehrke is believed to have been killed while leading his men although his body was never found. His place as brigade commander was taken by Major Wilhelm Weidenbrück who had been with the brigade since its formation (1).

In the last days of October 1944 the brigade was thrown into a night attack undertaken in support of the tanks of 6.Panzer-Division but the Soviets were able to beat back the German units which suffered heavy losses. On Wednesday, 1 November 1944 the brigade reported that twelve Panthers were available for operations while twelve were in repair, although it was expected that these would eventually return. On the following Friday, Major Weidenbrück was advised that the brigade was to be disbanded and the remaining equipment and personnel, with the exception of the staff, incorporated into 25. Panzer-Division (2).

Notes

1. Major Weidenbrück was awarded the Oakleaves to the Ritterkreuz for his leadership during the October fighting.

2. The order to consolidate the brigade staff with Panzergrenadier-Regiment 147 was never carried out and the remaining personnel were eventually used to form Panzer-Ausbildungs-Verband Ostee in March 1945.

Below: A Panther ausf G of 3.Kompanie, Panzer-Abteilung 2104 disabled during the fighting in Poland during the autumn of 1944. The very rough Zimmerit texture and the placement of the Balkenkreuz national insignia are both typical of Daimler-Benz produced vehicles. The flattened section of Zimmerit towards the front of the turret was almost certainly created to display a unit insignia and may have had some connection to Panzer-Regiment 9. This tank is also shown and discussed in the Camouflage & Markings section on page 19. At left: A Panther ausf G of Panzer-Regiment 9, 25.Panzer-Division photographed in Czechoslovakia in April 1945. A similar method of displaying both the division's unit insignia, at the front of the turret, and the regiment's, at the centre, can be seen here. The latter was only adopted after November 1944 and was based on the name of the commander, Oberst Eberhard Zahn, who had previously served with Panzer-Brigade 101 and Panzer-Regiment 21 and so is unlikely to have been used by Panzer-Abteilung 2104.

THE SECOND GENERATION
PANZER-BRIGADEN 105-110

On 24 July 1944 a new instruction was issued that confirmed the anticipated dates by which the formation of the first ten Panzer brigades was to be completed. This order also conferred the honour title Feldherrnhalle on Panzer-Brigaden 106 and 110 but did not introduce any other major changes. On 26 July 1944 the KstN documents and corresponding establishments set out below are mentioned for the first time in an order outlining the formation of Panzer-Brigaden 109 and 110. On 6 August 1944 new orders were issued regarding the organisation of Panzer-Brigaden 105-110, adding a number of Sdkfz 251/21 halftracks to the headquarters of the Panzer battalion and increasing the size of the Panzergrenadier element from three to five companies. It was planned that the earlier brigades would be reorganised at some later date but it would seem that this never came about.

Stab Panzer-Brigade	Stabs-Kompanie einer Panzer-Brigade

Nachrichten-Zug	Erkunder-Zug	Aufklärung-Zug	Grosse Kraftwagenkolonne (60t) KstN 1231 von 1.11.1943

The brigade headquarters was made up using parts of KstN 1104a (gp) von 1.4.1944 Stab und Stabskompanie eines Panzergrenadier-Regiments ausf A (gepanzert). The initial 7 July 1944 proposals give two Sdkfz 251/3 halftracks and this was retained in the 18 July revisions. The Stabskompanie was built using the Gruppe Aufklärung-Zug from KstN 1107b (fG) v 1.4.1944, a preliminary amendment to the Panzer battalion establishment superseded by an order of 1 June 1944. The 7 July 1944 proposals suggested three 251/1, four 251/3, three 251/7 and three 251/11 halftracks for the Stabskompanie but the exact breakdown is unknown at this time. The Erkunder-Zug, a light scouting unit, was based on KstN 1150 (fG) von 1.4.1944 and contained four Truppen. With the units shown above, the 18 July orders listed the following for the entire Stab und Stabskompanie: 1. An Aufklärungs-Zug, or armoured reconassaince platoon. 2. An Erkunder-Zug made up of four sections. 3. A Sanitätsstaffel , or medical evacuation section. 4. A Gefechtstross, or armament and ammunition supply section.

The repair and recovery unit was based on KstN 1151a (fG) von 1.4.1944 Versorgungs-Kompanie Panzer-Abteilung 'Panther' (frei Gliederung). This unit, with two Bergepanthers, may not have been authorised for the early brigades but the vehicles were certainly on hand with Panzer-Brigaden 105-108. Under the command of the recovery unit was an anti-aircraft platoon based on parts of KstN 1150 (fG) v 1.9.1944 Stabskompanie einer Panzer-Abteilung (freie Gliederung).

Stab Panzer-Abteilung (frei) KstN 1107a(fG) von 1.4.1944	Panzer-Fla-Zug (frei) KstN 1196(fG) von 1.4.1944

3 x Panzerbefehlswagen V

4 x FlakPz IV 3.7cm

Panzer-Kompanie 'Panther' (frei) KstN 1177(fG) von 1.4.1944	Panzer-Kompanie 'Panther' (frei) KstN 1177(fG) von 1.4.1944	Panzer-Kompanie 'Panther' (frei) KstN 1177(fG) von 1.4.1944	Panzerjäger (Sturmgeschütz) Kompanie KstN 1149(fG) von 1.4.1944

11 x Pzkpfw V   11 x Pzkpfw V   11 x Pzkpfw V   11 x Jagdpanzer IV

Stab Panzergrenadier-Bataillon (frei) KstN 1108a(fG) von 1.4.1944	Panzer-Pionier-Kompanie KstN 714 von 1.6.1944	Versorgungs-Kompanie (frei) KstN 1151a(fG) von 1.4.1944

The organisation of the Panzer-Pionier-Kompanie is examined in greater detail in the section dealing with the third generation brigades.

1.Kompanie	2.Kompanie	3.Kompanie	4.Kompanie	5.Kompanie

It is almost certain that the first and second companies were formed using KstN 1114c(gp)(fG) von 1.7.1944 Panzergrenadier-Kompanie (gepanzert) (frei Gliederung) oder Panzer-Aufklarungs-Kompanie (gepanzert) (frei Gliederung). The late George Tessin, an authority on the organisation of the Wehrmacht, gives the KstN number as 1114c and the date as 1.4.1944 but includes the July description which also allows for the formation of a reconnaissance company. But there is no listing for any version of KstN 1114 dated from April 1944 in the surviving files of the Allgemeines Heeresamt and I feel that may have been assumed. Both companies were reorganised from 1 August 1944 as KstN 1114b(gp)(fG) Panzergrenadier-Kompanie (gepanzert) (frei Gliederung) and KstN 1114d(gp)(fG) Panzergrenadier-Kompanie (MG 151-20 Drilling) (gepanzert) (frei Gliederung) which introduced the Sdfkz 251/21 but reduced the overall number of standard halftracks.

The third company was probably organised using KstN 1121a (gp) (fG) v 1.4.1944 Teileinheit Führer einer schweren Kompanie (gepanzert) (freil Gliederung). That is parts of KstN 1121a acting as the command of the third company. There is no record of a KstN for this date in the Allgemeines Heeresamt list but it is mentioned by Tesssin.

The fourth company was made up of two part units built around KstN 1126(gp) von 1.4.1944 Teileinheit 12cm Granatenwerfer Zug (gepanzert). There is no record of this KstN in the Allgemeines Heeresamt list but it may have been a late or temporary addition. The suffix frei Gliederung, which is often quoted, is almost certainly incorrect.

The battalion's fifth company was based on KstN 1125(gp)(fG) von 1.4.1944 Teileinheit 7.5cm schwere Kanone Zug (gepanzert) (frei Gliederung).

Overall the second generation brigades were better organised and equipped that the first generation units although they were still deficient in basic transport vehicles. Brief histories of Panzer-Brigaden 105-110 are presented on the following pages.

This Panther ausf G of Panzer-Brigade 105, commanded by the brigade adjutant, was disabled near Eynhatten in September 1944. The camouflage pattern seems to have been common to the tanks of Panzer-Abteilung 2105 and was made up of large patches of Olivgrün outlined in Rotbraun. This tank is also shown on page 19 of the Camouflage & Markings section.

Panzer-Brigade 105. Formed on 24 July 1944, the brigade was made up from parts of the badly depleted 18.Panzergrenadier-Division and drafts from various armoured training units. The brigade's Panzer-Abteilung 2105, under the command of Hauptmann Horst Hanemann, was established at Bamberg under the auspices of Panzer-Ersatz-Abteilung 35 and was trained on the Pzkpfw V Panther at Bamberg and Erlangen (1). The first tanks were allocated on 7 August 1944 and by the end of the same month the last nine Panthers were shipped from the Heereszeugamt bringing the battalion's total to thirty-six, although it is unclear when the actual deliveries took place (2).

The eleven Panzer IV/70 (V) tank destroyers, which were to equip the fourth company of the Panzer battalion, were not despatched until 1 September 1944 and by the time the company was able join the brigade it had been at the front for some time. In addition to the difficulties experienced with the supply of heavy equipment, very little time was given over to training and a number of company commanders did not reach their units until the second half of August.

During the first week of September 1944 the brigade was transferred by rail to the area between Brussels and Namur in Belgium and was immediately caught up in the general retreat. The tanks of Panzer-Brigade 105 went into combat for the first time on 7 September under the command of 7.Armee in an attack made east of Leuven, close to Brussels. Subsequently the brigade took part in the battles in eastern Belgium, most notably in the defence of Fleron and in a counterattack at Malmedy. From mid-September the brigade supported 9.Panzer-Division in the fighting on the Westwall south of Aachen, losing over half the Panzergrenadier battalion.

On 23 September 1944 the brigade was disbanded and most of the survivors were integrated into the units of 9.Panzer-Division except the headquarters staff of the Panzer battalion and the men of the Versorgungs company which were merged with the remnants of Panzer-Abteilung 2113 to form II.Abteilung, Panzer-Regiment 10.

Panzer-Brigade 106. Formed on 24 July 1944 and initially commanded by Oberst Dr. Franz Bäke, one of the German army's most capable soldiers, the brigade began its training at Truppenübungsplatz Mielau in Poland, north-east of Warsaw. Parts of the brigade staff, the supply company and the Panzergrenadier battalion were taken from Panzer-Regiment 11 and the Ersatzheer, or replacement army, but much of the combat elements were built around the remnants of Panzergrenadier-Division Feldherrnhalle and Panzer-Ersatz- und Ausbildungs-Abteilung Feldherrnhalle and the brigade also received the title (3). The first eleven Panthers arrived at the battalion on 1 September 1944 and a further twenty-five had been shipped for the Heereszeugamt by 19 August, although it is not clear when these arrived. The first units left the training areas on 30 August 1944 and within a week the

Notes

1. On 22 September 1944 Hanemann was seriously wounded and replaced by Hauptmann Siegfried Krüger.

2. Several accounts, including that of Major Heinrich Volker the brigade commander, suggest that as many as fifty Panthers were on hand with the battalion. These are almost certainly incorrect and the allocations taken from the official records show the following shipments: 7 August, eight tanks; 8 August, nineteen tanks, and; 21 August, nine tanks.

3. The honour title Feldherrnhalle was originally bestowed on Infanterie-Regiment 271 in 1942 in recognition of the large number of former Sturm-Abteilung (SA) men within its ranks. During the war a number of army units received the title, including 13.Panzer-Division and schwere Panzer-Abteilung 503, but by 1944 the connection with the SA had largely been lost.

Notes

1. Many accounts state that Stabsfeldwebel Oskar Moser of the Panzer battalion's 2.Kompanie was a fourth recipient but his Ritterkreuz was awarded for a much earlier action when Moser was a platoon commander with Panzer-Abteilung 160.

majority of the brigade had been transferred to the Western Front. The Panzer battalion's 4.Kompanie could have spent little or no time in training as their Panzer IV/70 (V) tank destroyers were not shipped from the Heereszeugamt until 29 August 1944 and the company is known to have been involved in the brigade's first battle. From 7 September the brigade took part in the defensive operations at Briey, south-west of Thionville, and the withdrawal towards Trier where the Panthers were able to destroy twenty-six American tanks and armoured cars in a single action near Oberkorn on the French-Luxembourg border. However, these initial actions were extremely draining and in its first day of combat alone the brigade lost twenty-one tanks and tank destroyers and over sixty halftracks.

On Thursday, 14 September 1944 the brigade supported 3.Panzergrenadier-Division in an attack against the Moselle bridgehead south of Metz which continued until the following Sunday.

The brigade remained in this area until the end of the month when it was moved first to Saint-Dié-des-Vosges, north-west of Colmar, and then to Belfort. In late October Panzer-Brigade 106 supported a Kampfgruppe made up from 21.Panzer-Division and 16.Volksgrenadier-Division in a counterattack near Raon where the Americans had broken through the German defensive line near Mortagne.

During November 1944 the brigade was involved in defensive actions as part of the operational reserve of 1.Armee along the so-called Falkenberg Line, south-east of Metz, and also at Bechingen and Saint-Avold. In a counterattack undertaken north of Sélestat, between Strasbourg and Colmar, on the last two days of the month, elements of Panzer-Brigade 106 claimed the destruction of thirty-five enemy tanks, seven of which were knocked out by Gefreiter Josef Fink, a squad leader of Panzergrenadier-Bataillon 2106 using a Panzerschreck. Gefreiter Fink was later awarded the Ritterkreuz for his actions, one of only three men of the brigade to receive the medal (1).

In the first weeks of December 1944 the brigade took part in the counterattacks at Sigolsheim and At Château du Haut-Königsbourg on the northern edge of the Vosges and also of the defensive line around of Kayserberg-Vignoble, north of Colmar.

On 8 December the brigade reported that four Jagdpanzers were on hand together with just ten Panthers, of which as few as five may have been combat ready. At least one account states that two Pzkpfw IV tanks were also with Panzer-Abteilung 2106 but I feel that these may in fact be the vehicles grouped with a number of Panthers and Pzkpfw III tanks into a Kampfgruppe under Hauptmann Paul te Heesen, the Panzer battalion commander, which later supported the last of the

............continued on page 14

Photographed near Malry, west of Metz, this Panther ausf G of 3.Kompanie, Panzer-Abteilung 106 was disabled during the German counterattack which began during the late evening of 7 September 1944. This tank is also shown in the Camouflage & Markings section on page 20.

Panzer-Brigade 106 Feldherrnhalle ended the war fighting in western Germany and this Panther ausf A model was probably one of the last tanks operated by Panzer-Abteilung 2106 before it was incorporated into Panzer-Division Clausewitz. The tank was originally abandoned in the city centre of Bonn near the approach to the Hindenburgbrücke, which the retreating Germans destroyed on 8 March 1945, and later moved about 150 metres to the south along Doetschstrasse.

The wreckage of an Sdkfz 251/21 Drilling halftrack photographed near Keintzheim in December 1944. the unit insignia of Panzer Brigade 106, based on the Feldherrnhalle Rune, can be seen on the rear hull. The second generation Panzer brigades were each authorised forty-two of these vehicles.

The Panther ausf A of Panzer-Abteilung 2106 shown in the photograph above in front of the Beethoven-Halle in Brückenstrasse, just over 100 metres from the west bank of the Rhine, shortly after the city was occupied by the US Army. It is likely that this tank could not be moved due to a mechanical failure or lack of fuel as the Germans evacuated Bonn without offering any resistance. From here it was moved to Doetschstrasse and in later images it seems that the Zimmerit has been completely removed. Note the hooks on the turret sides which held lengths of spare track.

............continued from page 12

Notes

1. I should perhaps mention here that most of the unit histories in this book were compiled using German sources, many of them wartime documents and narratives, and, where possible, I have changed the place names to their modern-day versions. In a number of cases these are significantly different and I apologise for any confusion this may cause.

2. At least one account states that the number of Panther tanks never exceeded thirty-three.

Jagdpanther tank destroyers of schwere Panzerjäger-Abteilung 654. After the battles around Kayserberg the brigade was withdrawn to Soultz-Haut-Rhin, north of Mulhouse, and held in reserve but had returned to the front by the middle of January to take part in the counterattacks on the Alsace bridgehead (1).

Also at this time Oberst Bäke left the brigade and was briefly succeeded by Major Bernhard von Schkopp until 24 January 1945 when Oberstleutnant Heinrich Drewes could make his way to the West from Danzig where he had been in charge of Ersatz-Brigade Feldherrnhalle.

For much of late February and early March the remnants of the brigade operated in small Kampfgruppen based for the most part on the survivors of the Panzer and Panzergrenadier battalions with an assortment of vehicles that may have been scraped together for other units. In early April the brigade was trapped in the Ruhr Pocket and although most of the personnel surrendered there to the Americans, a significant number managed to escape.

On 14 April 1945 Panzer-Brigade 106 received ten Panther tanks and, three days later, the surviving elements were incorporated into the newly raised Panzer-

Division Clausewitz. On 22 April 1945, after taking part in the heavy fighting near Langeleben, east of Brunswick, the last elements of Panzer-Abteilung 2106 were disbanded.

Panzer-Brigade 107. The formation of this unit began on 24 July 1944 at the Mielau training grounds in Poland with most of the personnel coming from the badly depleted 25.Panzergrenadier-Division and the Ersatzheer. The brigade's tank battalion, Panzer-Abteilung 2107, was led by Major Hans-Albrecht von Plüskow and was drawn from Panzer-Abteilung 125, Reserve-Panzer-Abteilung 8 and various training and replacement establishments of Wehrkreis V.

On 24 August 1944 the first eleven Panthers were allocated by the Heereszeugamt with a further eight on 27 August and the last seventeen on the following day. Although this represents the brigade's full authorisation of thirty-six tanks it is unclear when these arrived while the Panzer IV/70(V) tank destroyers that were to equip 4.Kompanie were not shipped until 8 September (2). The brigade commander, Major Berndt-Joachim Freiherr von Maltzahn, had been promised a period of at least nine to twelve weeks to complete the brigade's training but on

This Befehlspanzerwagen V Panther ausf G, commanded by Major Hans-Albrect von Plüskow, the Abteilungsführer of Panzer-Abteilung 2107, was disabled near Erp, north-east of Eindhoven, on 23 September 1944 by a British Sherman tank. The brigade operated three of these command vehicles and the other command tanks were probably allocated to Major Berndt-Joachim Freiherr von Maltzahn, the brigade commander, and Leutnant Graf Von Brockdorff-Ahlefeld, one of Plüskow's company commanders. As part of Kampfgruppe Walther the battalion's Panthers were advancing towards the road between Veghel and Uden at around noon when a 75mm anti-tank round fired from the rear slammed into the left track quickly followed by two more which hit the turret, killing Major Plüskow. A reconstruction of how this tank may have appeared before it was extensively damaged is shown on page 22.

This Panther ausf G of 2.Kompanie, Panzer-Abteilung 2107 attached to Panzer-Brigade 107 was disabled during the fighting around the town of Overloon on the Meuse river south of Nijmegen in late September 1944. Another view of this vehicle can be seen on page 2 and it is also shown in the Camouflage & Markings section on page 23. This tank was left in the same location for many years but was later restored is today on exhibit at the Nationaal Oorlogs- en Verzetsmuseum just a short distance from where it was recovered.

4 September 1944 OKW advised that the training period was at an end. While this was not unusual for the independent Panzer brigades it meant that most of Plüskow's tank crews had been given a week or less to familiarise themselves with their vehicles.

On Friday, 15 September 1944 the brigade began entraining for the Western Front and was originally promised to 5.Panzerarmee in Belgium, which was preparing a counterattack towards Aachen, but by Sunday afternoon the decision had been made to move the brigade to the area between Arnhem and Nijmegen to oppose the Allied airborne landings that had taken place that morning as part of Operation Market Garden.

On 19 September, while parts of the brigade were still being unloaded at Venlo, the tanks of Panzer-Abteilung 2107, with the paratroopers of Fallschirmjäger-Regiment 21 on board, moved off to capture the bridge over the Wilhelmina Canal at Son. Led by Leutnant Cay-Lorenz Graf Von Brockdorff-Ahlefeld, one of Plüskow's company commanders, the Panthers attacked the American position at Son in the early afternoon and although they met with some initial success they were unable to force their way across the canal and as darkness fell the attack was called off. In the early hours of the following morning, 20 September 1944, Maltzahn sent the infantry of Panzergrenadier-Bataillon 2107 against

the American positions hoping to take the bridge by surprise but within an hour was once again forced throw his tanks into the battle. Just as the Americans seemed to be on the verge of giving way a number of British Cromwell tanks arrived to take the Panthers in the flank, leaving four of the German tanks burning on the approaches to Son and blunting the German attack. Maltzahn was forced to withdraw his men to Nuenen, some 3 kilometres to the south-west, and taking advantage of this the British reinforced the Allied position with a complete tank regiment and managed to clear the main road to Nijmegen by noon.

But later that afternoon the tanks of Panzer-Brigade 107 were able to first hold an Allied counterattack made towards Nederwetten and then throw the British tanks and American paratroopers back as far as Eindhoven. That evening Maltzahn learnt that two strong British armoured forces were advancing from the south and had in fact made contact with the US paratroopers at Geldrop, just 3 kilometres from his positions around Nuenen. Fearing that his only escape route would soon be closed Maltzahn ordered his men to fall back towards Helmond. As the brigade was pulling back through the gap between Gerwen and Stiphout, during the early morning hours of 21 September, the British advance guard caught up with the Germans. A fierce firefight ensued and although the brigade reached Helmond another three irreplaceable tanks were left

Notes

1. Commanded by Oberst Erich Walther, a Fallschirmjäger officer, the composition of this Kampfgruppe changed several times during the battle. It contained at one time or another units of the army, the Waffen-SS and even a Luftwaffe penal battalion that arrived directly from the Mediterranean and fought in their tropical uniforms.

2. Volker, it will be remembered, had commanded Panzer-Brigade 105 until it was disbanded on 23 September 1944.

3. Similarly the loss of three Panthers, which must have been destroyed after the 19 September battle, is not explained.

on the battlefield. That night Maltzahn was ordered to move to Gemert, about 8 kilometres further to the north, and join Kampfgruppe Walther which was preparing an attack to break through the Allied corridor between Eindhoven and Nijmegen at Veghel (1).

Just before noon on the Friday, 22 September 1944, under the cover of a thick haze, the infantry of Kampfgruppe Walther advanced towards Erp, 4 kilometres southeast of Veghel, followed by the Panthers of Panzer-Brigade 107. Pushing aside the defences of a US airborne unit the tanks reached the road at a point between Veghel and Uden and turned towards the south. Although the corridor was now effectively cut the Germans could only manage an advance of a few kilometres and were stopped in front of Veghel by a scratch force of American paratroopers that were continually reinforced during the day. In the late afternoon the Panthers of Panzer-Brigade 107 made a last attempt to capture the town but were pushed back by a regiment of British tanks and although sporadic fighting continued into the hours of darkness, the Germans were unable to go any further.

The brigade suffered heavy losses in this single day of fighting including Major von Plüskow, the commander of Panzer-Abteilung 2107, who was killed instantly when the turret of his command Panther was struck by an anti-tank round. A subsequent Allied counterattack was unable to exploit their success and on 24 September 1944 the brigade was withdrawn, once again, to Gemert. On the next day Maltzahn was ordered to moved the remnants of his brigade to the area around Overloon and Oploo to defend the Maas River crossing at Boxmeer. At this time the brigade reported that nineteen Panthers were on hand with just seven tank destroyers and Flakpanzers available for immediate deployment. Faced by the overwhelming strength of the US 7th Armored Division the Germans abandoned Oploo and although Allied attacks at Overloon and Venlo were halted the brigade suffered significant losses, particularly the Panzergrenadier battalion.

By the end of October 1944 the brigade had been reduced to a weak battle group with just eleven Panthers, the equivalent of one full tank company, and eight Jagdpanzers remaining. Major von Maltzahn was blamed, quite unfairly, for the brigade's lack of success and replaced by Major Heinrich Volker (2) and the remnants of Panzer-Brigade 107 were withdrawn to Truppenübungsplatz Baumholder, 20 kilometres north-west of Kaiserslautern, on 8 November 1944 and disbanded on the following day.

Panzer-Brigade 108. Commanded by Oberstleutnant Friedrich-Heinrich Musculus, the formation of this unit began on 24 July 1944 at Grafenwöhr in Germany with the brigade headquarters and many of the other elements created from the personnel of Panzer-Regiment 39. The brigade's tank battalion, Panzer-Abteilung 2108, was raised from men of the Ersatzheer.

The first eight Panthers were allocated on Thursday, 24 August 1944 and by the following Monday a further twenty-eight tanks had been shipped to the battalion by the Heereszeugamt. The official records here are incomplete and it is unclear when the tanks arrived although the authorised number of thirty-six were on hand by 18 September 1944 when the brigade started moving to the front. The eleven Panzer IV/70 (V) Jagdpanzers of the battalion's 4.Kompanie were not shipped until the next day and they are not mentioned in the brigade's reports until the first week of October by which time the Panzer battalion had been in combat for two weeks.

Elements of the brigade arrived at the front late on 18 September and Oberstleutnant Musculus was ordered to prepare his men for a counterattack in support of the Panzer-Lehr-Division at Hüttingen against US armoured units that had broken through the Westwall defences between Bitburg and Wallendorf. That night, on the approach to their start lines, ten Panthers broke down and when the attack went in early on the following day a further fifteen tanks were badly damaged of which ten were complete write-offs. In addition, the tank battalion commander, Major Kempf, his signals officer and two of his platoon leaders were killed.

Despite these losses the attacks continued for the next three days until the brigade was withdrawn and transferred to the command of II.Fallschirmkorps which was defending the area south-east of Arnhem on the edge of the Reichswald. On 4 October 1944 the brigade reported that twenty-three Panthers were on hand although just twelve of these were considered combat-ready. The same report mentions that a total of eight Panzer IV/70 (V) tank destroyers were with 4.Kompanie which suggests that the company had joined the brigade some days prior to this date as three vehicles had already been lost (3).

On 7 October 1944 the brigade was moved to the Aachen area and on the following day took part in a counterattack towards Alsdorf with the Tigers of schwere Panzer-Abteilung 506. The initial attack went well but by 9 October much of the Panzergrenadier battalion had been cut off in the town of Bardenburg, 6 kilometres

............continued on page 49

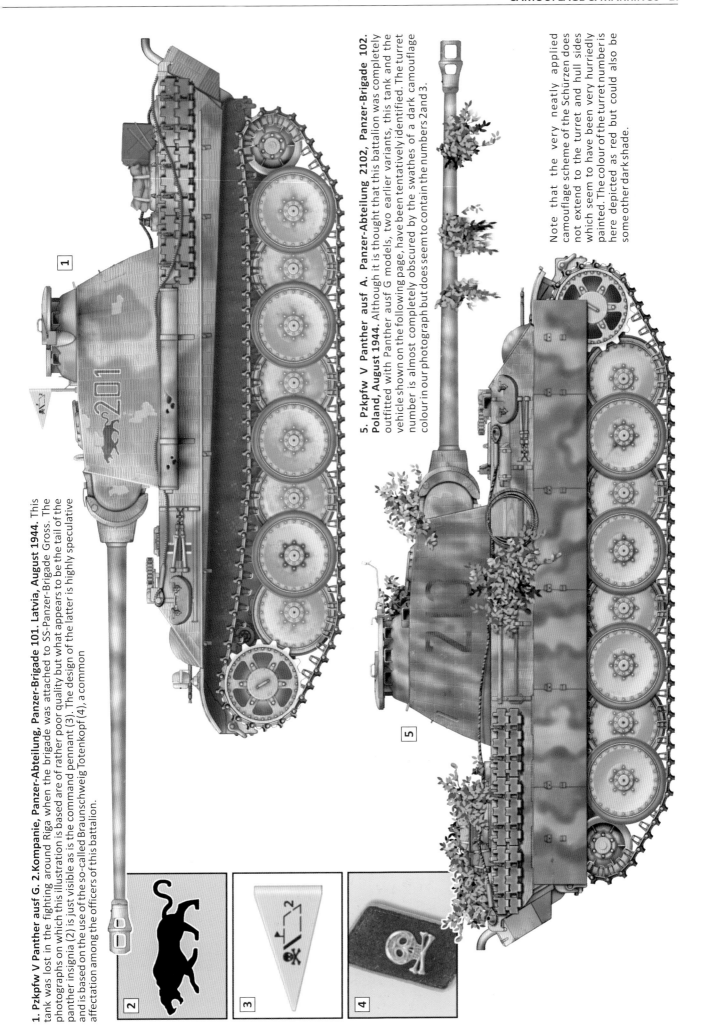

1. Pzkpfw V Panther ausf G. 2.Kompanie, Panzer-Abteilung, Panzer-Brigade 101. Latvia, August 1944. This tank was lost in the fighting around Riga when the brigade was attached to SS-Panzer-Brigade Gross. The photographs on which this illustration is based are of rather poor quality but what appears to be the tail of the panther insignia (2) is just visible as is the command pennant (3). The design of the latter is highly speculative and is based on the use of the so-called Braunschweig Totenkopf (4), a common affectation among the officers of this battalion.

5. Pzkpfw V Panther ausf A. Panzer-Abteilung 2102, Panzer-Brigade 102. Poland, August 1944. Although it is thought that this battalion was completely outfitted with Panther ausf G models, two earlier variants, this tank and the vehicle shown on the following page, have been tentatively identified. The turret number is almost completely obscured by the swathes of a dark camouflage colour in our photograph but does seem to contain the numbers 2 and 3.

Note that the very neatly applied camouflage scheme of the Schürzen does not extend to the turret and hull sides which seem to have been very hurriedly painted. The colour of the turret number is here depicted as red but could also be some other dark shade.

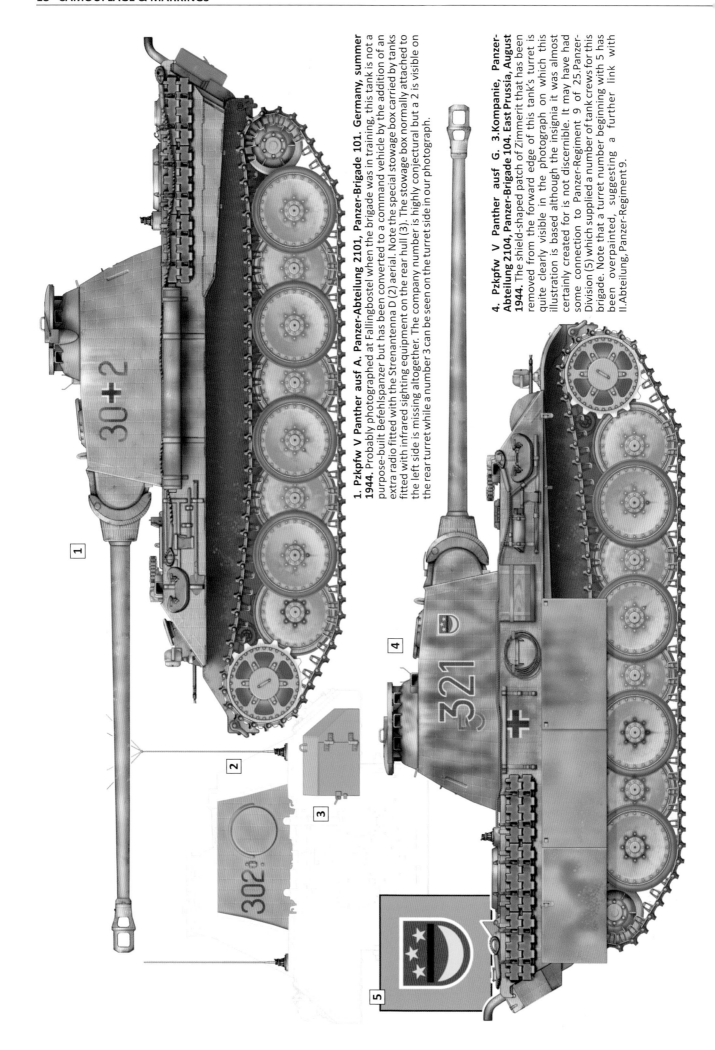

1. Pzkpfw V Panther ausf A. Panzer-Abteilung 2101, Panzer-Brigade 101. Germany, summer 1944. Probably photographed at Fallingbostel when the brigade was in training, this tank is not a purpose-built Befehlspanzer but has been converted to a command vehicle by the addition of an extra radio fitted with the Strenantenna D (2) aerial. Note the special stowage box carried by tanks fitted with infrared sighting equipment on the rear hull (3). The stowage box normally attached to the left side is missing altogether. The company number is highly conjectural but a 2 is visible on the rear turret while a number 3 can be seen on the turret side in our photograph.

4. Pzkpfw V Panther ausf G. 3.Kompanie, Panzer-Abteilung 2104, Panzer-Brigade 104. East Prussia, August 1944. The shield-shaped patch of Zimmerit that has been removed from the forward edge of this tank's turret is quite clearly visible in the photograph on which this illustration is based although the insignia it was almost certainly created for is not discernible. It may have had some connection to Panzer-Regiment 9 of 25.Panzer-Division (5) which supplied a number of tank crews for this brigade. Note that a turret number beginning with 5 has been overpainted, suggesting a further link with II.Abteilung, Panzer-Regiment9.

1. Pzkpfw V Panther ausf G. Stab, Panzer-Abteilung 2105, Panzer-Brigade 105. Belgium, September 1944. This tank, commanded by the battalion adjutant Oberleutnant Vennemann, was disabled as it attempted to conduct a rearguard action through the town of Eynatten, south of Aachen. The camouflage pattern made up of large Olivgrün shapes outlined in Rotbraun was common, if not universal, throughout the battalion. Note that the turret number has been painted over the Balkenkreuz national insignia.

2. Pzkpfw V Panther ausf G. 2.Kompanie, Panzer-Abteilung 2105, Panzer-Brigade 105. Belgium, September 1944. Photographed near Eupen, close to the German border, this tank is coated in Zimmerit in the pattern indicative of MNH produced vehicles, as most of the battalion's Panthers were. Note that most of the roadwheels have been camouflaged in the same manner as the turret and hull, a practice which was actively discouraged. The barrel appears very dark in our photograph (3) and may be a recent replacement or simply badly burnt.

1. Pzkpfw V Panther ausf G. 3.Kompanie, Panzer-Abteilung 2106, Panzer-Brigade 106 Feldherrnhalle. France, September 1944. The tanks of this battalion used the standard three-digit system of numbering applied with a stencil. The number is shown here as a pale yellow but may have been another light colour. The outline was almost certainly in black. The pattern of Zimmerit is typical of MAN-assembled Panthers as most of the battalions' tanks seem to have been. Note the use of fencing wire to hold foliage camouflage on the barrel. This tank was abandoned and captured almost intact after the fighting around Metz.

2. Pzkpfw V Panther ausf G. 3.Kompanie, Panzer-Abteilung 2106, Panzer-Brigade 106 Feldherrnhalle. France, September 1944. Also photographed after the battles around Metz, this tank may be another example of a standard vehicle converted in the field to a command tank as suggested by the Sternantenna D. There is no evidence that the Feldherrnhalle unit insignia (3) was carried on any of the battalion's Panthers but it certainly was used by other elements of the brigade (4). It is included here as a matter of interest only.

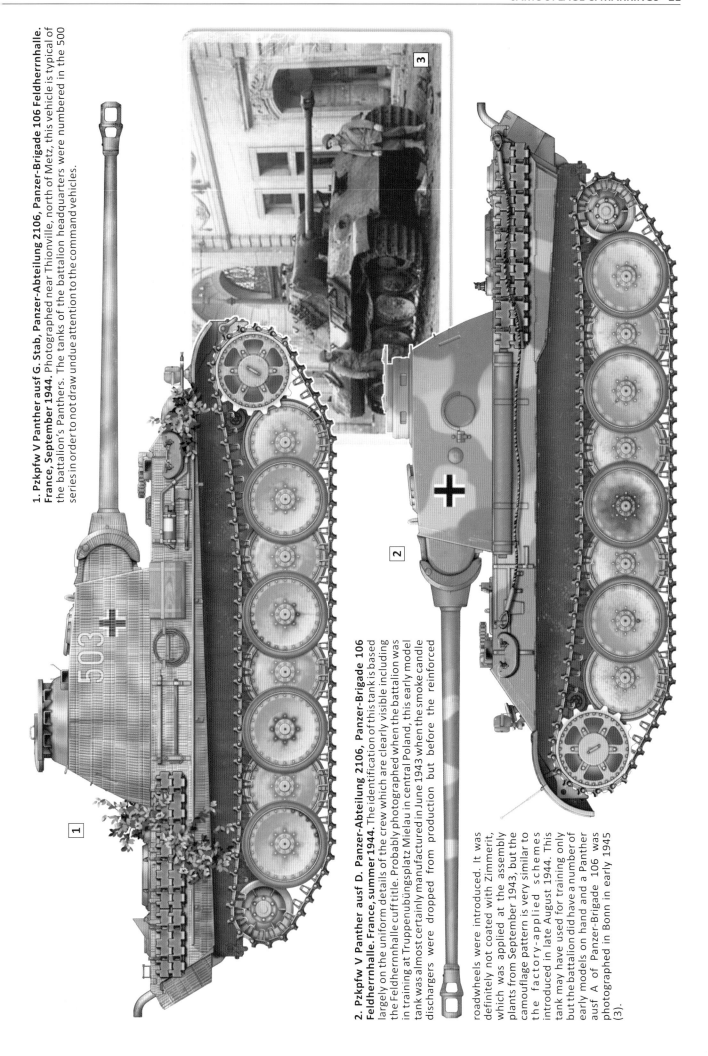

1. Pzkpfw V Panther ausf G. Stab, Panzer-Abteilung 2106, Panzer-Brigade 106 Feldherrnhalle. France, September 1944. Photographed near Thionville, north of Metz, this vehicle is typical of the battalion's Panthers. The tanks of the battalion headquarters were numbered in the 500 series in order to not draw undue attention to the command vehicles.

2. Pzkpfw V Panther ausf D. Panzer-Abteilung 2106, Panzer-Brigade 106 Feldherrnhalle. France, summer 1944. The identification of this tank is based largely on the uniform details of the crew which are clearly visible including the Feldherrnhalle cuff title. Probably photographed when the battalion was in training at Truppenübungsplatz Mielau in central Poland, this early model tank was almost certainly manufactured in June 1943 when the smoke candle dischargers were dropped from production but before the reinforced roadwheels were introduced. It was definitely not coated with Zimmerit, which was applied at the assembly plants from September 1943, but the camouflage pattern is very similar to the factory-applied schemes introduced in late August 1944. This tank may have used for training only but the battalion did have a number of early models on hand and a Panther ausf A of Panzer-Brigade 106 was photographed in Bonn in early 1945 (3).

1. **Pzkpfw V Panther ausf G. 1.Kompanie, Panzer-Abteilung 2107, Panzer-Brigade 107. Holland, September 1944.** The two Balkenkreuz markings, one of which is partly covered by the turret number, were a common feature of this battalion's Panthers. Several theories have been put forward as to why this may have been necessary but none are particularly convincing and we will probably never know the true reason. Although the photograph on which this illustration is based is of mediocre quality, the centre of the turret number is significantly lighter than the black of the Baleknkreuz markings and may have been rendered in red or green

2. **Befehlspanzerwagen V Panther ausf G. Stab, Panzer-Abteilung 2107, Panzer-Brigade 107. Holland, September 1944.** The battalion operated three of these purpose-built command vehicles during the fighting in Holland when Panzer-Brigade 107 was attached to Kampfgruppe Walther. Most of the Zimmerit is missing in our photograph and the turret number 002, although possible, is largely conjectural and is based on what appears to be a large number 2 on the turret rear (3). The battalion commander, Major Hans-Albrect von Plüskow, was killed when this tank was disabled on 23 September 1944 near Erp, north-east of Eindhoven, by a British Sherman.

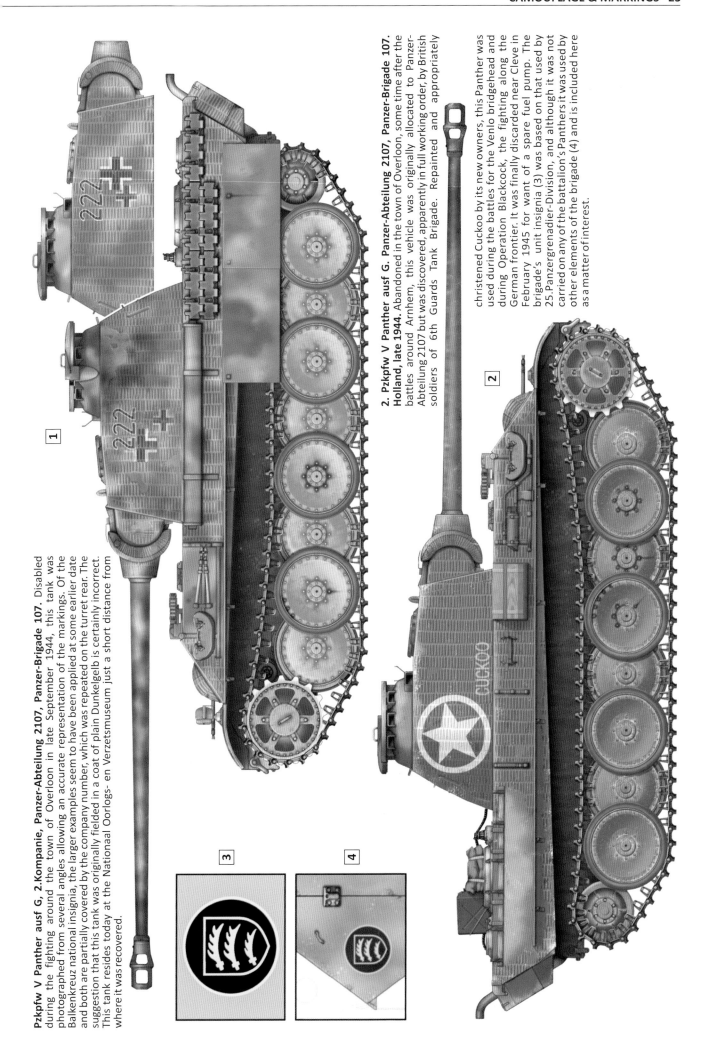

Pzkpfw V Panther ausf G, 2.Kompanie, Panzer-Abteilung 2107, Panzer-Brigade 107. Disabled during the fighting around the town of Overloon in late September 1944, this tank was photographed from several angles allowing an accurate representation of the markings. Of the Balkenkreuz national insignia, the larger examples seem to have been applied at some earlier date and both are partially covered by the company number, which was repeated on the turret rear. The suggestion that this tank was originally fielded in a coat of plain Dunkelgelb is certainly incorrect. This tank resides today at the Nationaal Oorlogs- en Verzetsmuseum just a short distance from where it was recovered.

2. Pzkpfw V Panther ausf G. Panzer-Abteilung 2107, Panzer-Brigade 107. Holland, late 1944. Abandoned in the town of Overloon, some time after the battles around Arnhem, this vehicle was originally allocated to Panzer-Abteilung 2107 but was discovered, apparently in full working order, by British soldiers of 6th Guards Tank Brigade. Repainted and appropriately christened Cuckoo by its new owners, this Panther was used during the battles for the Venlo bridgehead and during Operation Blackcock, the fighting along the German frontier. It was finally discarded near Cleve in February 1945 for want of a spare fuel pump. The brigade's unit insignia (3) was based on that used by 25.Panzergrenadier-Division, and although it was not carried on any of the battalion's Panthers it was used by other elements of the brigade (4) and is included here as a matter of interest.

1. Pzkpfw V Panther ausf G. Panzer-Regiment 24. Belgium, late 1944. When Panzer-Brigade 108 was disbanded in October 1944 the remnants were incorporated into Panzer-Regiment 24. Most of the Panthers of this regiment could usually be identified by several modifications including the removal of the tube for the gun cleaning rods from the hull side to the rear deck and the fabrication of metal racks which were fitted to the rear plate next to each stowage box to hold jerry cans. In addition, the distinctive unit insignia of the former 24.Kavellerie-Division was prominently displayed on the left-hand stowage box. None of these features are present in our photograph and the tank is coated in Zimmerit which fixes its production date to early September 1944 at the latest. Although far from certain, this may be one of the surviving Panthers of Panzer-Brigade 108, perhaps the least photographed of all the independent Panzer brigades.

2. Pzkpfw V Panther ausf G. 4.Kompanie, Panzer-Regiment 16, Panzer-Brigade 111. France, September 1944. Photographed during the fighting for Arracourt, east of Nancy, the camouflage of this tank is typical of the brigade's Panthers with heavy bands of Olivgrün overlaid with irregular shapes of Rotbraun on a base coat of Dunkelgelb. The numbering system was consistent throughout the battalion and was applied using stencils. Although the resulting gaps were sometimes filled by hand many were not, as shown in our example. Our photograph (3) depicts the same vehicle and illustrates the extensive use of foliage camouflage.

1. Pzkpfw V Panther ausf G. 3.Kompanie, Panzer-Regiment 29, Panzer-Brigade 112. France, September 1944. Photographed in the town of Dompaire, west of Épinal, this vehicle is typical of the MAN manufactured Panther ausf G tanks of Panzer-Brigade 112. The large numbers seem to have been used by most, if not all, the tanks of 3.Kompanie and were almost certainly rendered in black with a white outline as depicted here, although another dark colour is possible. This Panther is today on display at the Muséum des Blindés de Saumur in France.

2. Pzkpfw V Panther ausf G. 1.Kompanie, Panzer-Regiment 29, Panzer-Brigade 112. France, September 1944. The Heereswaffenamt advised that henceforth tanks would be painted in a specified camouflage scheme before they left the factories. The Panthers manufactured by MAN and MNH were painted in the manner shown here, the so-called disc pattern, until the end of September. As Zimmerit was discontinued at the beginning of that month, very few tanks could have been finished in the disc-pattern and coated with the anti-magnetic mine paste but many seem to have been allocated to Panzer-Brigaden 111, 112 and 113. This MNH-produced tank is also shown in our photograph (3) and the discs are clearly visible on the gun mantlet. The factory-applied schemes are examined in some detail in *Panther Tanks: German Army and Waffen-SS Defence of the West, 1945*, the eighteenth book in this series.

1. Pzkpfw V Panther ausf G. 2.Kompanie, Panzer-Regiment 130, Panzer-Brigade 113. France, September 1944. Disabled during the Arracourt battles, this Panther is also painted in a version of the factory-applied camouflage scheme that was in use by MAN and MNH briefly from late August until the end of September 1944.

Other photographs of this tank show that it has the turret splinter guard, Pilze sockets on the turret roof, driver's rainguard, late welded exhaust and the so-called horizontal ladder-style Zimmerit indicating it was assembled in late August 1944 by MNH. The style of company number, where a rough outline of Dunkelgelb has been applied, was common throughout the battilon with slight variations.

2. Pzkpfw V Panther ausf G. 3.Kompanie, Panzer-Regiment 130, Panzer-Brigade 113. France, September 1944. This MNH-produced tank was also disabled in the fighting near Arracourt and is marked in the same style as the Panther shown above. The camouflage pattern may be a very early factory-applied scheme or it may have been painted by the unit's workshop. Note the special stowage box (3) for the infrared sighting equipment on the rear hull which is just visible in our photograph (4).

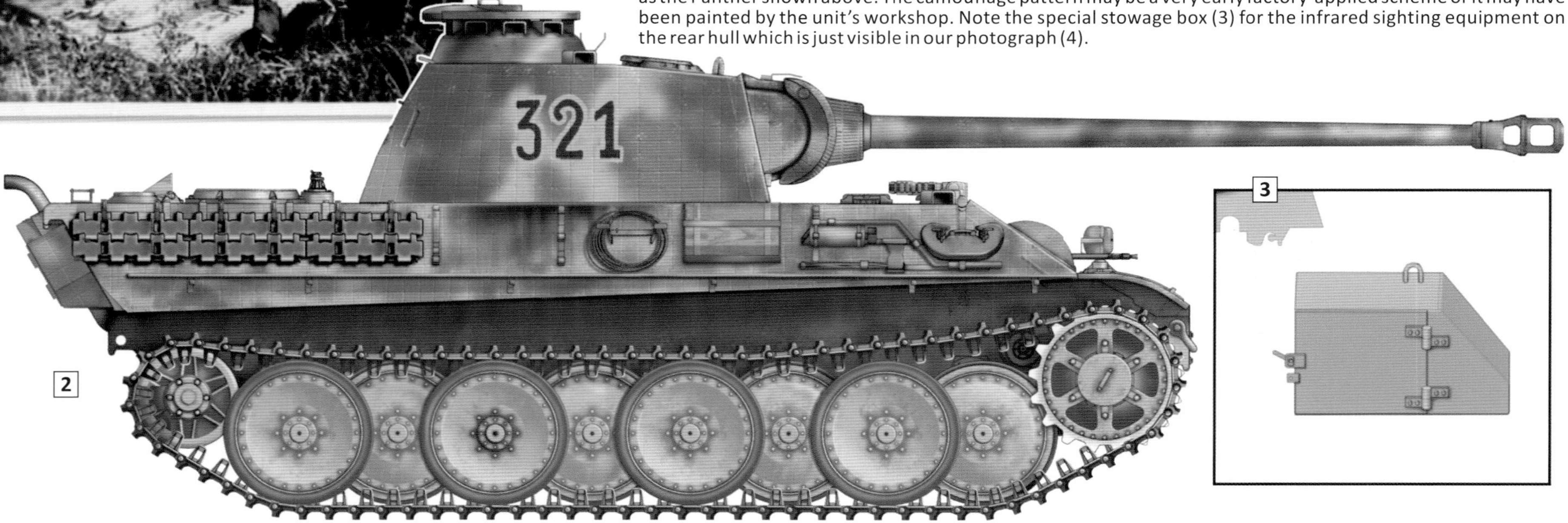

PANTHER AUSF A
1/35 SCALE
ALEXANDER PEDAN

Alexander's Panther ausf A is based on a Dragon Models kit with Zimmerit paste created using Revell modelling putty. The barrel is a milled aluminium part from Eduard Model Accessories and the early exhausts are marketed by Mosquito. The completed model was painted with Tamiya acrylics and weathered using oil paints and MIG pigments

A rear view of the completed model. The stowage boxes on the rear hull and tool clasps are photo-etched brass details from Eduard Model Accessories and Aber. The crew figures are from Russian company Tank Figures and Accessories and were painted in a mixture of acrylics, oil paint and tempera.

ERSATZ M10 PANTHER AUSF G

PANZER-BRIGADE 150
1/35 SCALE
ERIC D. WISDOM

American modeller Eric D. Wisdom's model depicts one of the disguised Panther ausf G tanks that took part in the Ardennes Offensive in late 1944. Eric used the Dragon Models' 1/35 scale kit with Fruilmodel metal tracks, a Voyager Model photo-etched upgrade set, a new barrel from RB Model and a drive sprocket from Panzer Art. All these companies have been featured in this series. The images below show the added photo-etched parts, simulated battle damage on the fabricated sheet metal hull front and the model in the early stages of painting and weathering.

Views of the completed model showing the extensive weathering, with very realistic mud and grass, and the fake US Army markings. The XY code was applied to all these vehicles to identify them to German military field police. This model will eventually take its place in a diorama and Eric envisioned it as not one of the five known Ersatz tanks but as one of the additional five that are mentioned in some accounts, hence the damage to the hull front.

PANTHER AUSF G
PANZER-BRIGADE 106
1/35 SCALE
DU WEI JIE

Singaporean modeller Du Wei Jie's Panther ausf G is based on a Dragon Models' 1/35 scale kit Nr.6384 first released in 2009. Although the kit is quite accurate, a number of small details have been added or refined such as the towing cable, the spare tracks on the hull side and the hatch handles.

The Zimmerit texture is indicative of MAN-produced vehicles and this tank is also shown and discussed in the Camouflage & Markings section of this book on page 21. The markings of Panzer-Abteilung 2106 are included in the kit.

Shown above, at left, is the Kugelblende machine-gun mount and the travel lock for the main gun. At right is the jack block, fire extinguisher and other tools.

Below: The commander's cupola with anti-aircraft machine gun attachment and a view of the rear deck showing the photo-etched brass covers and towing cable shackle.

Above: The driver's hatch, gun travel lock and driver's periscope and, at right, a rear view of the turret showing details of the cupola periscopes, and the Zimmerit coating. The slightly rough appearance, including some areas of damage, and the scale of the ridges and grid, are thoroughly realistic. This model was also featured in Panther Tanks: German Army and Waffen-SS Normandy Campaign 1944, *the third book in this series, but space restrictions did not allow us to present a comprehensive coverage at that time.*

The Pzkpfw V Panther tank is arguably one of the most famous armoured fighting vehicles produced during the Second World War and it has been a favourite with modellers and wargamers since 1961 when Tamiya and Airfix released plastic models of this tank in 1/35 and 1/76 scale respectively. Both would be considered rudimentary by today's standards but they were in fact far more accurate than a number of subsequent offerings and, rather surprisingly, the Airfix kit is still on the market although the Tamiya model has long since been superseded by more detailed and accurate representations.

The last few decades have seen a boom in the plastic model industry and kits of the Panther are currently available in sizes ranging from 1/285 scale wargames tanks to massive 1/6 scale radio-controlled vehicles. As a consequence there are far too many to list here individually and, as with the other books in this series, I have chosen to concentrate on the most popular modelling scales of 1/35 and 1/48, although I have tried to include some of the smaller scale models. As many manufacturers regularly withdraw products from their catalogues, often only to be repackaged and re-released at some later date, I have tried to include models which are readily available at the time of writing and where this is not so I have tried to make it clear.

As this title, for the most part, fills a gap in the time period between *Panther Tanks: German Army and Waffen-SS Normandy Campaign, 1944* and *Panther Tanks: German Army and Waffen-SS Defence of the West, 1945,* I have endeavoured to include versions of the Panther which would have been the most commonly encountered during the battles of the late summer and the autumn of 1944. Similarly, I have purposely omitted models specifically marketed as having factory modifications which were incorporated after September 1944 and I would refer those readers interested in the earlier or later versions to the volumes mentioned above. Finally, the reader should note that for this chapter I have used the word Type in place of the more correct Ausführung, as at least one major manufacturer does, solely to avoid confusion. An index of manufacturers, with their contact details, can be found on page 64.

TAMIYA INC

This Japanese company is currently the largest producer of scale model kits in the world, having begun life as a sawmill and timber supply firm. In 1959, after some success with wooden models, the company switched to injection moulded plastic and in 1961 released its first armoured vehicle kit, a motorised Panther.

By the early 1970s Tamiya was producing a large range of armoured vehicles, with complementary figures and accessories, and was almost solely responsible for the rise in popularity of 1/35 scale. Although rather basic by today's standards, these kits were highly accurate and detailed when compared to what else was available at the time. Importantly, they were all made to the same scale, encouraging modellers to build a collection, and affordable. The company's near monopoly of the

1/35 scale market remained unchallenged until the release of the first Dragon Models kits in 1987. The current catalogue lists a Type A, which is an older kit lacking some detail and features of the newer releases, an early Type G, in both a static and motorised version, and an early Type G with a photo-etched Zimmerit stencil. In 2003 Tamiya began releasing a series of models in 1/48 scale and this line has been extremely successful for the company, combining the potential for a high level of detail without the expense of the bigger kits.

The sole 1/48 scale offering at the time of writing is a later Type G which lacks the Zimmerit texture common to most of the tanks allocated to the Panzer brigades. Tamiya also produces radio-controlled models of a Type G in both 1/35 and 1/16 scale.

Below, right: Tamiya's large 1/25 scale Panther Type G. At left: Zimmerit texture in 1/35 scale sold separately and workable track, also in 1/35 scale. Note that the latter are the early variety without cleats.

DRAGON MODELS LTD

This Hong Kong-based company took the plastic model industry by storm in the late 1980s with the release of their first 1/35 scale kits and Dragon is still known for its innovative approach. The company's small scale kits are some of the best available. At the time of writing this company offered seven construction kits in both 1/35 and 1/72 scale representing variants of the Panther tanks that served in the North-west European campaign including a Type D, a Type A and an early Type G, all with Zimmerit texture. The smaller scale kit of the early Type G includes a number of well-detailed and anatomically-correct crew figures. The company also produces a kit of one of the Panther Type G tanks that were disguised as American M10 tank destroyers and used during the Ardennes Offensive. In addition to these, Dragon produces a pre-painted early Type G in 1/72 scale although the model lacks Zimmerit and is finished in markings that, while pleasing, are not completely accurate.

Below: Details of Dragon Models' Panther Type G including the Bosch headlight, hull glacis with Zimmerit coating and the rear hull plate.

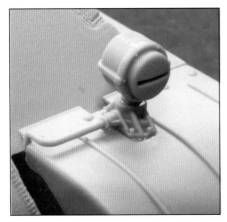
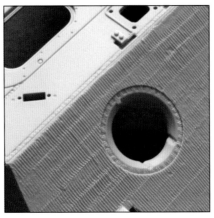
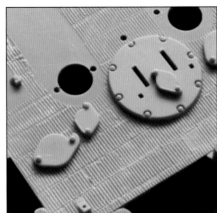

TAKOM

One of the newest model manufacturers, this company started operating in Hong Kong in 2013 as Takom World and shortly afterwards expanded to open a plant in mainland China where all the models are now produced. Most kits are in 1/35 scale and the company offers models of the early, mid and late production versions of the Panther Type A and Panther Type D models both with and without Zimmerit. All these models have detailed interiors and come with optional transparent parts for the hull and turret. All this detail comes at a price of course and Takom models are relatively expensive when compared to Dragon and Tamiya. Takom also produces two Bergepanther kits in 1/35 scale.

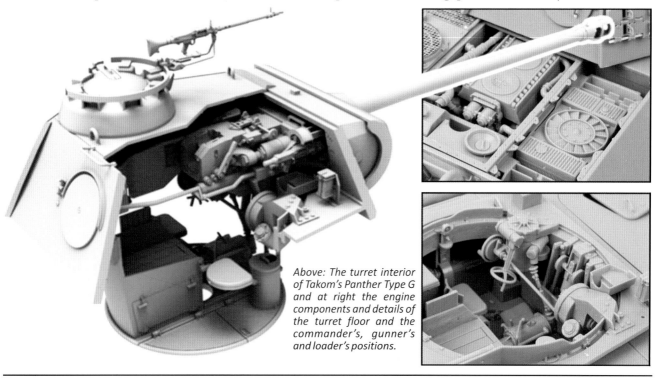

Above: The turret interior of Takom's Panther Type G and at right the engine components and details of the turret floor and the commander's, gunner's and loader's positions.

MENG-MODEL

This Chinese company largely specialises in modern armour but also produces a number of Second World War subjects including a Panther Type A and Panther Type D, the latter with and without Zimmerit. The box of the Panther Type D also carries the logo of the Bovington Tank Museum, implying their cooperation, although I have been unable to confirm this. As I have mentioned in a previous book, a visit to the company's website, as with many Chinese model manufacturers, can be an exercise in frustration with the products listed here under the names of various dinosaurs. Meng also offers sheets of Zimmerit texture in the patterns employed by MAN and MNH in 1/35 scale for the Panther Type A.

Below: Meng-Model's recently-released Bergepanther recovery tank in 1/35 scale. The 3.7cm anti-aircraft gun, positioned on the hull front, is rarely seen in contemporary photographs.

Far left: The 1/35 scale Panther Type A model. The large beam, held in place by a metal rack, on the rear deck was indicative of the tanks of SS-Panzer-Regiment 5 but is easily omitted during construction.

RYE FIELD MODELS

Based in Hong Kong, this company released its first armour models, three highly accurate and detailed kits depicting Tiger I variants, within the short space of six months from late 2015. Rye Field Models also offers a Panther Type D and a Panther Type G, the latter being a very recent release. Both can be built as early or late production vehicles and the Panther Type G contains over 1,500 plastic parts, 196 photo-etched parts and 190 individual track links and track pins. The kit also contains a number of optional clear plastic parts to allow the detailed interior to be viewed. Shortly after the release of this model a cheaper, less detailed, version was marketed at a considerably reduced price. It seems strange that some kind of Zimmerit coating is not included with either model although the marking options allow for a vehicle in service in June 1944 in Normandy.

Above: Rye Field Models' Panther Type G in 1/35 scale with and without full interior. Below: Details of the Panther Type G kit with full interior option. Although the company maintains that this model can be built as an early production version, the addition of Zimmerit paste would be required to more accurately represent a tank assembled prior to early September 1944, as most of those allocated to the Panzer brigades were.

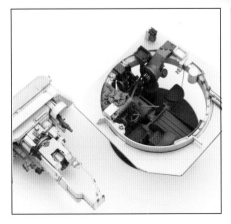

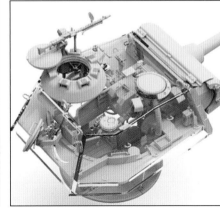

REVELL & AIRFIX

Revell is one of the oldest firms involved in the plastic model industry, tracing its roots back to the Precision Specialties company that was founded in 1943. Like Airfix, Revell has gone through many changes of ownership over the intervening years and was at one time operated as two distinct entities in the USA and Germany with two quite different catalogues. The company's current offerings include a 1/72 Panther Type G and Panther Type A and although these are both good kits, readers should be aware that the commander's cupola should have seven periscopes and not six, an inexplicable error in otherwise accurate models. The Airfix 1/76 scale Panther, a Type G model, was first released in 1961 and although the box art may have been altered over the years, the kit itself remains unchanged, including the rubber band tracks which seem to be impervious to any known glue.

Below: Revell's Panther Type G in 1/72 scale, built and painted as a later production version by the author.

At far right: Three incarnations of the Airfix 1/76 scale Panther. It should be mentioned that, contrary to the implications of the artwork, no Panthers were sent to North Africa.

TRUMPETER/HOBBY BOSS

Often thought to be separate entities, these Chinese companies are in fact owned by the same corporation, are located at the same address and are essentially the same firm although different models are marketed separately under the two labels. Hobby Boss produces a 1/16 scale early production Panther Type G, which actually depicts a tank assembled in September or October 1944, and a Panther Type A with Zimmerit in 1/35 scale. The 1/35 scale Panther Type D Flak Bergepanther model utilised the hull and suspension of the Panther Type A kit fitted with a 3.7cm gun.

The Trumpeter/Hobby Boss Panther Type A in 1/35 scale built with the photo-etched brass upgrade set from Tetra Models. Zimmerit is supplied with the kit, in a pattern very similar to that seen on DEMAG-assembled vehicles, in the shape of fifty-one thin plastic sheets.

E.T. MODEL

This company, based in China, produces upgrade sets in 1/72 and 1/35 scale in brass and resin. Although most sets are specifically designed, according to the company, to fit Dragon or Tamiya kits, some parts or accessories, for example the stowage bin, are referred to as universal. Shown below is the Tamiya 1/35 scale kit built with E.T. Model's upgrade set and details of Dragon Models' 1/72 scale Type G model finished with E.T. Models photo-etched brass set.

Above: Details of E.T. Models 1/72 scale upgrade set for the early production Panther Type G. Below: Meng-Model's 1/35 scale Panther Type A built with E.T. Model's photo-etched brass upgrade set.

Below: A late model Panther Type G in 1/35 built by Penny Shi using E.T. Model details. This tank is of a much later version than the vehicles covered in this book but the fittings for the tools, the stowage boxes and the rack for the spare tracks are identical to those of the early production version.

VOYAGER MODEL

Voyager Model, based in Shanghai, have been manufacturing upgrade sets for scale models since 2003 with the release of their first set for 1/35 scale armour. The company produces a number of items in both 1/72 and 1/35 scale in photo-etched brass and also resin, including wheel hubs, damaged road wheels, ammunition crates and boxes and fuel containers. In addition Voyager also offers highly detailed and accurate milled aluminium and brass barrels and muzzle brakes. Although most of these details would be compatible with almost all manufacturers' models, some sets are marketed as appropriate for the specific kits from Tamiya, Dragon, Zvezda and ICM.

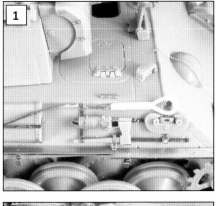
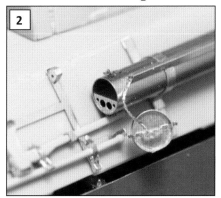

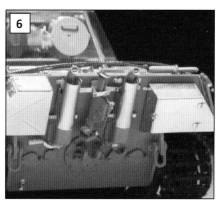

Above: Details of a number of 1/35 scale photo-etched brass upgrade sets from Voyager Model. 1. Tamiya Type G early production. 2. Dragon Models Type A later production showing the tube for the gun cleaning rods. 3. Dragon Type A later production. This image gives some idea of the large number of parts included in these sets. 4. Takom Type G showing the functioning stowage box lids. 5. Generic Schürzen and fender set. 6. Rye Field Models' Type G kit built with extra details from Voyager. This configuration, with a standard stowage box and special container for the infrared sighting equipment, is sometimes seen on the Panther tanks operated by the Panzer brigades and is mentioned in the Camouflage & Markings section.

ROYAL MODEL

Founded in the early 1990s, this Italian company produces high-quality accessories and aftermarket parts in metal and resin. The catalogue includes complete upgrade sets for both the Dragon early and late Type A, the Tamiya Type G and the Italeri Type A, all in 1/35 scale. Royal Model also offers photo-etched brass hull Schürzen for the Type A and G which are appropriate for all 1/35 scale kits. Other 1/35 scale items include two interior detail sets for the Type A and photo-etched Zimmerit for the Type A, either factory fresh or damaged. More generic parts in resin and brass are an engine transmission, detailed rear stowage bins, engine grills and a Kugelblende machine gun mount.

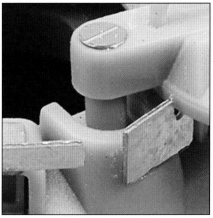
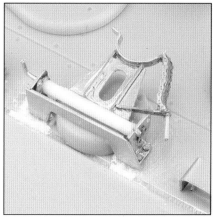

Above, from left to right: Examples of the very high standard of detail incorporated into Royal Model's 1/35 scale upgrade sets. Shown here are the tool bracket for the hull left-hand side, the locking mechanism of the commander's cupola hatch in the open position and the gun travel lock for a Panther Type A or Type D.

EDUARD MODEL ACCESSORIES

Founded in 1989, this Czech company produces high quality upgrade kits in photo-etched metal and resin and a number of scale models. Currently available are extensive photo-etched detail sets to update the Tamiya Panther, including sets of Zimmerit produced in the patterns typical of MAN and MNH-manufactured vehicles, the Zvezda Type and the Dragon Type G and late Type A. The company also offers vinyl masks to aid with painting the roadwheels. At the time of writing all the 1/48 and 1/72 scale sets for the Panther had been discontinued. The recently-released Type G kit from Tamiya includes a photo-etched Zimmerit set from Eduard.

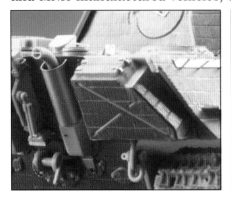
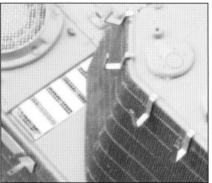

Above and at left: Tamiya's 1/48 scale Panther Type G built with the extensive Eduard photo-etched brass set which includes the MAN pattern Zimmerit coating.

Below: Dragon Models' 1/35 scale Panther Type G built with Eduard Model Accessories photo-etched brass set. Of note are the very fine buckles and clasps of the tools and the accurate brackets holding the hull Schürzen.

RB MODEL

RB Model from Poland produce a range of milled aluminium and brass gun barrels and resin accessories for 1/72, 1/48 and 1/35 scale armour models. Shown below is the beautifully detailed 1/35 scale barrel and muzzle brake for the 7.5cm KwK 42 L/40 gun which armed the Panther. More generic items include highly detailed towing shackles, radio antenna insulators and fuel drums.

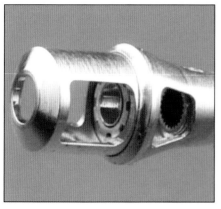

ABER

This Polish company has been manufacturing and selling upgrade sets since 1995, working in photo-etched brass, milled aluminium, stainless steel and even wood. For some time now Tamiya has included a number of Aber products with their models. A full list of the accessories made specifically for the Panther in all scales would be far too large to reproduce on this page, particularly in light of the company's regular new releases, and the reader can find the company's contact details on page 64.

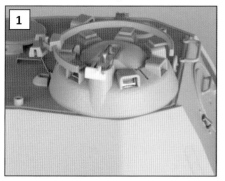
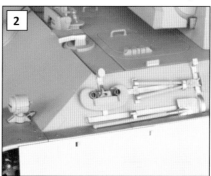

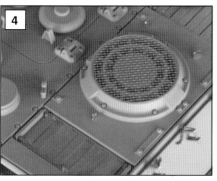

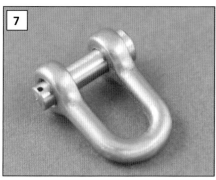
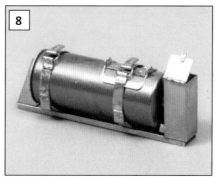
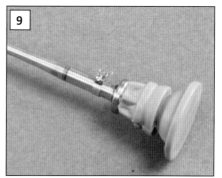

Above: A selection of Aber parts and details, all in 1/35 scale unless noted. 1. Turret cupola from the Panther Type G Basic Set. 2. Tool rack from the same set. 3. Rear stowage box for a Panther Type G. 4. Photo-etched metal engine air intake grill. 5. Tamiya's 1/48 scale Panther Type G built with Aber's upgrade set. 6. Barrel and muzzle brake for the 7.5cm gun in aluminium and brass. 7. An early model towing shackle. 8. A standard fire extinguisher in its bracket. 9. A command wireless antenna and insulator.

GRIFFON MODEL

This Chinese company produces a large range of photo-etched brass sets for the Panther Type A and Type G in 1/35 scale to fit most manufacturers' kits, although they do recommend Tamiya and Dragon.

All the photographs reproduced here show details of the upgrade sets for the Dragon Models Panther Type G early version which was the most common version in service with the Panzer brigades.

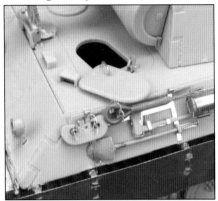 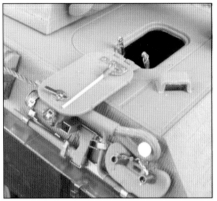 

Above, left to right: Details of Griffon Model's upgrade sets in 1/35 scale for the Panther Type A or D, the Panther Type G and the tube holding the cleaning rods for the 7.5cm gun and the aerial extensions indicative of Befehlspanzerwagen command tanks. Below: Dragon Models' 1/35 scale Panther Type A built as a command tank with the upgrade set from Griffon Model.

Below: Dragon Models' 1/35 scale early production Panther Type g with Zimmerit with photo-etched brass parts from Griffon. The same model showing the rear stowage box, sheet metal guards for the exhaust muffler and additional parts for the jack.

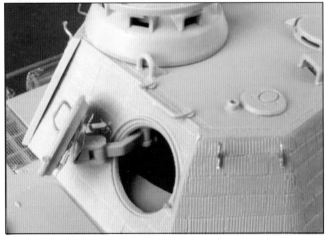 

MODEL ARTISAN MORI

This small Japanese company produces resin upgrade parts for 1/35 scale armour models including detailed commander's cupolas and stowage boxes for the infrared sight equipment for the Panther. They also produce more general items such as crew uniforms and tool sets, including fire extinguishers, tow shackles and bolt cutters. Shown below, are: 1. The Panther drive sprocket with a selection of hub caps. 2. The early cast armoured exhaust covers. 3. The gun mantlet.

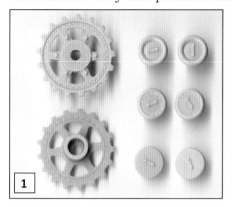
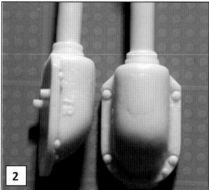
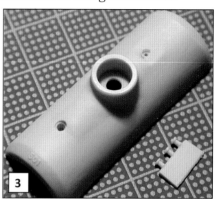

ROCHM MODEL

This company is owned and managed by master modeller Sheng Hui, whose work has appeared in a number of books in the TankCraft series, and specialises in 1/35 scale detail sets in resin, photo-etched brass and aluminium. After extensively covering the Tiger I, the company moved onto the Tiger II series and then the Panther, currently offering forty-five different upgrade sets as part of a program titled Evolution of the Panther which is intended to continue into the very last production models. Although the detail sets are marketed a specific to Dragon, Tamiya, Meng-Model and Takom models, many of the parts would of course be suitable for most 1/35 scale kits. At present these sets only cover the Type A and Type D versions of the Panther but the range expands on an almost daily basis. ROCHM Model's products offer exceptional detail and considering the quality, are reasonably priced. Detail sets in 1/48 and 1/72 scale are currently in the planning stage.

At right and below: Dragon Models' 1/35 scale Panther Type A fitted with photo-etched parts from ROCHM Model.

The high quality is obvious from the photographs and shown here is just a small selection of the hundreds of small parts in this set.

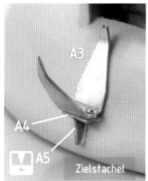

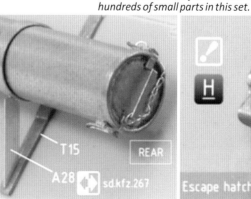

PANZER ART

Based in Poland, this company produces a large range of resin parts for Second World War and modern era armoured vehicles in 1/35 scale. Shown here, are: 1. Spare roadwheels. These are the later design with twenty-four reinforcing bolts. 2. The cast commander's cupola with interior detail including periscopes. 3. German wireless antenna insulators in two sizes.

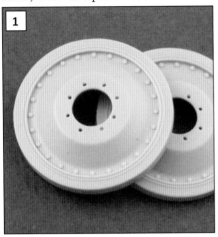
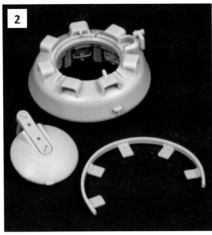
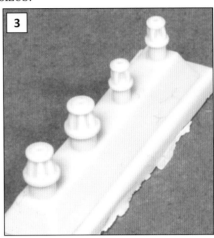

ARCHER TRANSFERS

Although most kits contain a choice of marking options I have included this company as a number their products relate specifically to the tanks mentioned in this book. Based in the United States, Archer Transfers began by marketing water slide transfers produced by Cartograf of Italy but probably best known for their range of dry, or rub-down, transfers. A set of these markings in 1/35 scale relates to the Panthers of Panzer-Brigade 113 and the finished product was the result of extensive research carried out by Ron Owen Hayes and Michael Bressanges. The company also offers four different sets of the so-called disc camouflage with thorough explanations of its development and instructions on applying the transfers to a scale model.

Below: Eric D. Wisdom's Panther ausf G partly completed with Zimmerit texture from Cavalier and Archer markings for 3.Kompanie, Panzer-Brigade 113. Further examples of Eric's work can be seen in the Model Showcase section of this book. At the bottom of the page, from left to right, are the complete Archer set for Panzer-Brigade 113, one of the disc camouflage sheets and the transfer applied to a 1/35 scale kit.

............continued from page 16

north of Aachen. An attempt to break through to Bardenburg made by Grenadier-Regiment 404 and the remaining tanks of Panzer-Abteilung 2108 on Tuesday, 10 October 1944 was ultimately unsuccessful but did relieve the pressure on the defenders. The Panzer battalion lost one of its tanks in this battle and that night the remaining six Panthers were withdrawn to Jülich, some 20 kilometres to the north-east.

At noon the next day, 11 October 1944, the surviving tanks of Panzer-Abteilung 2108 and five Panthers of 116.Panzer-Division renewed the attack towards Bardenburg but were held up at Würselen, less than 2 kilometres short of their objective. The acting commander of Panzer-Abteilung 2108, Hauptmann von Knöringen, was blamed for the failure of both relief attempts and subsequently arrested. The American tanks were able to secure Bardenburg that night and over the next few days days conducted a series of fierce counterattacks, pushing the Germans back to Geilenkirchen. The remnants of Panzer-Brigade 108 were withdrawn from the front line and with the units of 116.Panzer-Division were subordinated to the command of I.SS-Panzerkorps for the remainder of October.

The brigade was formally disbanded on 30 October 1944 after the fighting for Aachen with parts of the headquarters used to form Panzer-Brigade 150 while the remaining Panthers were handed over to I.Abteilung, Panzer-Regiment 24 of 116.Panzer-Division (1). The surviving tank destroyers were allocated to the division's Panzerjäger-Abteilung 228.

On 26 January 1945, the remaining command elements of Panzer-Brigade 108 were used to create the staff of Panzer-Regiment Coburg zbV (2) and it was ordered that three new companies be raised as Panzer-Abteilung 2108. Although two Panthers were allocated by the Heereszeugamt on 20 April 1945, both went to the second battalion of Panzer-Regiment 2 which was at that time defending the area north of Berlin against the Soviets. The companies of Panzer-Abteilung 2108 that had been reconstituted were absorbed by Panzer-Auffrischungs-Verband Krampnitz which was later subordinated to Panzer-Regiment 25 of 7.Panzer-Division.

Panzer-Brigade 109. The brigade's formation began on 24 July 1944 with the staff, motorised infantry and support elements established at Grafenwöhr in Germany utilising personnel and equipment from 25.Panzer-Division, 233.Reserve-Panzer-Division and various replacement units. At the same time the armoured component, Panzer-Abteilung 2109, was built up at Estergom in northern Hungary. The first Panthers were allocated on 8 August 1944 and by 18 September a total of thirty-six tanks had been received. As the units in Germany reached their established strength they were sent to Hungary and by the end of September the complete brigade had assembled at Truppenübungsplatz Orkenye, about 35 kilometres south-west of Budapest, where the last heavy weapons and the armoured halftracks were received. On 26 September 1944 a total of eleven Panzer IV/70(V) tank

Notes

1. The tank strength figures for this period are quite confusing with a report prepared for General der Panzertruppen West dated 19 October 1944 stating that Panzer-Abteilung 2108 was equipped with twenty Panther tanks at that time, eight of which were in short or long-term repair. The report also states that the battalion had lost a total eleven tanks in action. On 25 October 1944, I.Abteilung Panzer-Regiment 24 reported that twenty-nine Panthers were on hand but this figure had risen to forty-six within two days and we must assume that seventeen tanks were handed over from Panzer-Abteilung 2108 as no new allocations were made by the Heereszeugamt. I can offer no explanation as to where the vehicles mentioned in the 19 October report came from, the obvious discrepancy in the losses or why just seventeen tanks were taken over by Panzer-Regiment 24.

2. This unit is also discussed in connection with Panzer-Brigade 103.

Disabled and abandoned after the battles in Holland, this Panther ausf G is typical of the earlier production Panther ausf G models allocated to the independent Panzer brigades. Although large pieces of the Zimmerit coating have been broken off evidence of the so-called disc camouflage is still visible on the hull glacis. Note the Balkenkreuz national marking on the turret side. Examples of this camouflage pattern are shown on pages 25 and 26 of the Camouflage & Markings section of this book.

Photographed in Budapest in late 1945, this Panther ausf G is one of the tanks lost by 13.Panzer-Division during the defence of the city. Although it is impossible to be certain, the company number of 715 and the presence of Zimmerit would suggests that this may be one of the vehicles handed over from Panzer-Abteilung 2110.

Notes

1. The Hungarian government's secret negotiations to surrender to the Soviets had been discovered by the Germans. Operation Panzerfaust, conducted on 15 October 1944 by German troops, supported by a few Tigers, deposed the government and secured Hungary's continued support for the Axis cause.

2. The composition of this large ad-hoc formation, commanded by General Hermann Breith, changed frequently and at different times contained parts of 13.Panzer-Division and two Waffen-SS cavalry divisions.

3. The brigade's last commander, Oberstleutnant Joachim Helmut Wolff, would later be appointed to command the division during the siege of Budapest. The suggestion in some accounts that Panzer-Brigade 109 received the honour title Feldherrnhalle is incorrect.

4. Ersatz-Brigade Feldherrnhalle was the replacement depot for the Feldherrnhalle Panzergrenadier division and Marsch-Bataillon Feldherrnhalle was a convalescent unit.

destroyers were despatched from the Heereszeugamt and it seems likely that these arrived soon after. Some units of Panzer-Brigade 109 were engaged in combat at the end of September in local skirmishes at Keskemet and Tisza, south-east of Budapest, but the strongest elements of the brigade were held in reserve near the Hungarian capital in light of the precarious political situation (1).

With the arrival in Hungary of 24.Panzer-Division and the Tiger tanks of schwere Panzer-Abteilung 503, the brigade was released for operations at the front and on 11 October 1944 moved east through Hatvan to Debrecen, some 30 kilometres from the Romanian frontier, and joined Panzergruppe Breith (2). After a few indecisive actions the complete brigade was massed at Debrecen and on 16 October 1944 was able to cut off a Soviet breakthrough to the east of the town. Panzer-Brigade supported the tanks of 23.Panzer-Division here until 20 October when a general withdrawal was made to the Tisza River where Panzer-Abteilung 2109 defended the crossing at Tiszafüred. By the end of the month the brigade was fighting in the area around Nyiregyhaza, some 40 kilometres north of Debrecen, and had by this time lost much of its heavy equipment. On 5 November 1944 the remnants of Panzer-Brigade 109 were formally incorporated into Panzer-Division Feldherrnhalle (3).

Panzer-Brigade 110. Although orders were issued for the creation of this unit on 19 July 1944, the actual formation proceeded slowly and it was not until early August that the first elements were gathered at Truppenübungsplatz Warthelager near Poznan in Poland. Much

of the brigade staff, the Panzergrenadier battalion and the Panzer-Pionier company were drawn from Ersatz-Brigade Feldherrnhalle and Marsch-Bataillon Feldherrnhalle (4) and on 24 July 1944 the title was extended to the remainder of the brigade.

The brigade's armoured battalion, Panzer-Abteilung 2110, was formed from Panzer-Ersatz-Abteilungen 10 and 18, two training and replacement units based at Neuruppin and Böblingen respectively. The battalion's first tanks were shipped from the Heereszeugamt on 7 August 1944 but the full allocation was never achieved and the sixteen tanks received on 7 September 1944, bringing the battalion's total to thirty, would be the last vehicles issued. On 13 September 1944 a total of eleven Panzer IV/70 (V) tank destroyers were despatched to Hungary to equip the battalion's fourth company and although it is unclear when these arrived they were certainly on hand at the end of the month. By mid-August most of the brigade had been concentrated at Orkenye, near Budapest in Hungary, and was assigned to security duties while the last of the heavy weapons arrived including most of the Panzer battalion's tanks.

On 28 September 1944, just three days after the brigade's organisation was completed, the brigade commander, Oberstleutnant Wilhelm Schöning, was advised that Panzer-Brigade 110 was to be disbanded, its personnel and equipment used to rebuild 13.Panzer-Division. The Panthers of the Panzer-Abteilung became the fifth, sixth and seventh companies of the division's Panzer-Regiment 4 while the Panzer IV/70 tank destroyers were formed into a ninth company.

THE THIRD GENERATION PANZER-BRIGADEN 111-113

Formed in September 1944 the last three Panzer brigades were as strong in armour as a Panzer-Division but lacked the fighting reconnaissance elements and, perhaps most importantly, an organic artillery regiment. In fact all were understrength when they went into combat with most of the Panzergrenadier units making use of civilian cars in place of the authorised halftracks and Kettenkrad motorcycles. All three were virtually annihilated in their first actions and the establishments depicted here are based on official allocations and may not reflect the true state of affairs. Histories of each of the brigades are shown on the following pages.

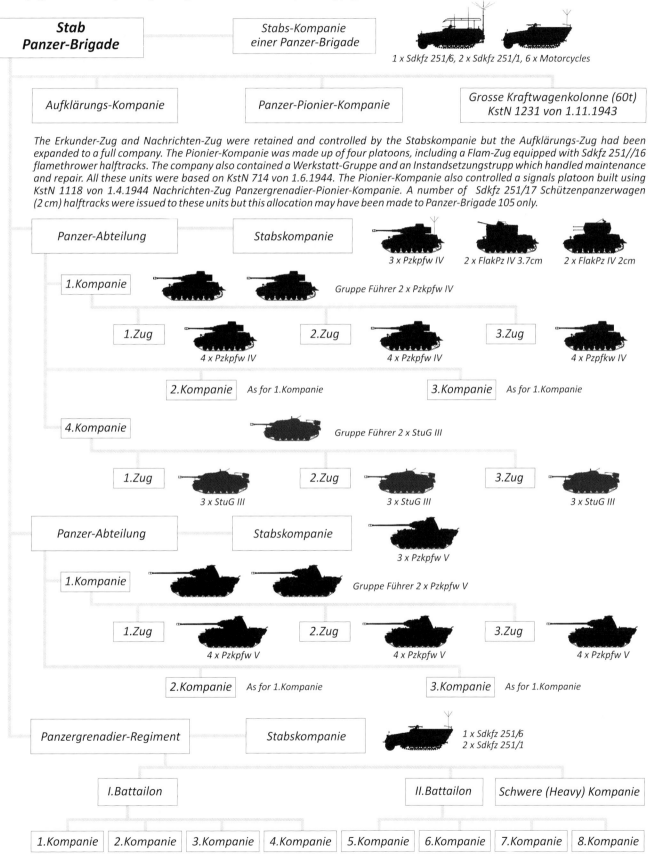

Stab Panzer-Brigade — Stabs-Kompanie einer Panzer-Brigade

1 x Sdkfz 251/6, 2 x Sdkfz 251/1, 6 x Motorcycles

Aufklärungs-Kompanie — Panzer-Pionier-Kompanie — Grosse Kraftwagenkolonne (60t) KstN 1231 von 1.11.1943

The Erkunder-Zug and Nachrichten-Zug were retained and controlled by the Stabskompanie but the Aufklärungs-Zug had been expanded to a full company. The Pionier-Kompanie was made up of four platoons, including a Flam-Zug equipped with Sdkfz 251//16 flamethrower halftracks. The company also contained a Werkstatt-Gruppe and an Instandsetzungstrupp which handled maintenance and repair. All these units were based on KstN 714 von 1.6.1944. The Pionier-Kompanie also controlled a signals platoon built using KstN 1118 von 1.4.1944 Nachrichten-Zug Panzergrenadier-Pionier-Kompanie. A number of Sdkfz 251/17 Schützenpanzerwagen (2 cm) halftracks were issued to these units but this allocation may have been made to Panzer-Brigade 105 only.

Panzer-Abteilung — Stabskompanie

3 x Pzkpfw IV — 2 x FlakPz IV 3.7cm — 2 x FlakPz IV 2cm

1.Kompanie — Gruppe Führer 2 x Pzkpfw IV

1.Zug 4 x Pzkpfw IV — 2.Zug 4 x Pzkpfw IV — 3.Zug 4 x Pzpfkw IV

2.Kompanie As for 1.Kompanie — 3.Kompanie As for 1.Kompanie

4.Kompanie — Gruppe Führer 2 x StuG III

1.Zug 3 x StuG III — 2.Zug 3 x StuG III — 3.Zug 3 x StuG III

Panzer-Abteilung — Stabskompanie

3 x Pzkpfw V

1.Kompanie — Gruppe Führer 2 x Pzkpfw V

1.Zug 4 x Pzkpfw V — 2.Zug 4 x Pzkpfw V — 3.Zug 4 x Pzkpfw V

2.Kompanie As for 1.Kompanie — 3.Kompanie As for 1.Kompanie

Panzergrenadier-Regiment — Stabskompanie

1 x Sdkfz 251/6
2 x Sdkfz 251/1

I.Battailon — II.Battailon — Schwere (Heavy) Kompanie

1.Kompanie — 2.Kompanie — 3.Kompanie — 4.Kompanie — 5.Kompanie — 6.Kompanie — 7.Kompanie — 8.Kompanie

The first three companies of each battalion contained three rifle platoons with one heavy weapons platoon equipped with 2 x 8.1cm mortars. The fourth company was a heavy support unit. The Schwere-Kompanie was attached directly to the regimental headquarters and was made up of 2 x 7.5cm howitzer sections, 2 x 12cm heavy mortar sections and 2 x 2cm towed anti-aircraft gun sections.

A Panther ausf G of 3.Kompanie, Panzer-Regiment 16 photographed in the streets of Bures in September 1944. The town of Bures lies between the Parroy forest and Arracourt and was used as a staging area for the German counterattacks. Note the Zimmerit coating and what may be a very early version of one of the factory-applied camouflage schemes.

Notes

1. The rank of Generalmajor, by which Schellendorf is referred to in many accounts, was conferred posthumously some time after October 1944. Many readers will be familiar with Valkyrie, or Walküre in German, as the codename used by the conspirators of the July 1944 plot to assassinate Hitler. The plan to mobilise the units of the Ersatzheer had in fact been formulated many months earlier and was used as a cover by the plotters.

2. An Armeegruppe was an ad-hoc formation that was larger than an Armee but not comparable in size to a Heeresgruppe.

Panzer-Brigade 111. From Saturday, 2 September 1944 elements of the new formation were gathered at Sennelager in Germany although the official formation date is usually given as the following Monday. Commanded by Oberst Heinrich-Walter Bronsart von Schellendorf, the brigade was made up in part from Panzer-Ersatz-Abteilung 11 and drafts from the Ersatzheer that had been created as part of the Valkyrie mobilisation programme (1). The three companies of Panzer-Abteilung 2111 were equipped with Pzkpfw IV ausf H or ausf J tanks and contained fourteen tanks each with a further three for the battalion staff. This gave a total of forty-five tanks and was a substantial increase in the number of vehicles authorised for the Panzer battalions of the first and second generation brigades. The anti-tank company was now organised as an assault gun battery and equipped with ten Sturmgeschütz III but was now directly subordinated to the brigade staff.

On 5 September 1944 Schellendorf was advised that the brigade was to move to the area around Épinal, south of Nancy in eastern France, and attached to Armeegruppe Blaskowitz (2). The German commander intended to use Panzer-Brigaden 111 and 113 in a counterattack against the US 3rd Army positions on the Moselle bridgehead.

On the same day I.Abteilung, Panzer-Regiment 16 was attached to the brigade and this unit retained the structure of a tank battalion of a Panzer regiment with three command tanks and three companies of fourteen tanks each. Between 24 August and 6 September 1944 a full complement of forty-five Panthers were allocated to the battalion by the Heereszeugamt and it seems that all were delivered before Panzer-Brigade 111 went into action. Although the Panzer units were well equipped, the Panzergrenadiers had none of their allocated halftracks and the few available trucks were used to move the support weapons into position. In addition, the lack of adequate recovery and repair facilities greatly hampered operations and by the time Panzer-Brigade 111 arrived in France the brigade headquarters reported that just six Pzkpfw IV tanks and nineteen Panthers were fully serviceable.

On 18 September 1944 the brigade, as part of LVIII.Panzerkorps, went into combat for the first time in an attack towards the town of Lunéville, about 20 kilometres south-east of Nancy, which was being held by elements of 15.Panzergrenadier-Division. The original plan for an assault in this area called for the participation of three Panzer brigades, two Panzer divisions and four Panzergrenadier divisions, including one Waffen-SS unit, all under strength at this time of the war but still a considerable force. In the event, as Lunéville was regarded as largely secured, only Panzer-Brigade 111 was employed. The brigade entered the town but become entangled in a bitter street fight and although the Germans inflicted heavy casualties on the Americans they were forced out again that night. An attack against Arracourt, some 10 kilometres further north, this time with the support of Panzer-Brigade 113 was planned for the next day but during the hours of darkness as the German units were moving into position, Panzer-Brigade 111 became lost. It seems that the reconnaissance units followed the directions of a local resident who deliberately misled them. In any case Panzer-Brigade 113 went into the attack alone and, hampered by the thick fog, was badly battered by the American defenders, losing over fifty tanks. Finally, on 20 September, Panzer-Brigade 111 was able to attack the American positions from the south causing some initial confusion but was eventually stopped after losing a number of tanks. On the next day both brigades were pulled from the front line and moved north to counter an American offensive that had driven a wedge between 1.Armee and 5.Panzerarmee but took over 24 hours to cover the 5 kilometres to their jump off positions.

From 22 September the Panzer brigades were thrown into an attack northwest of Chateau-Salin and with Panzer-Brigade 111 in the lead the German units were able to take advantage of the fog to advance to Juvelize-Arracourt but were inexplicably held up here for over three hours. When the fog cleared the Panzers were subjected to a hail of artillery fire and intense fighter-bomber attacks and Panzer-Brigade 111 was almost completely wiped out. By the end of the fighting just seven tanks were able to leave the battlefield under their own power and Oberst Schellendorf had been killed while leading his men.

On 1 October 1944 the brigade was officially dissolved and although it was planned to integrate the remaining elements into Panzer-Abteilung 115 (1), most of the survivors were absorbed by 11.Panzer-Division.

Panzer-Brigade 112. Formed on 4 September 1944 at the Grafenwöhr training grounds, this formation was also one of the units raised under the mobilisation of the Ersatzheer under the codename Valkyrie. The brigade was commanded by Oberst Horst von Usedom an experienced soldier who had served in Russia and Italy before taking up an appointment at the Fahnenjunker-Schule der Panzertruppen.

The brigade's Panzer-Abteilung 2112 reported that a full complement of Pzkpfw IV tanks were on hand in September and the tank destroyer company, referred to as Sturmgeschütz-Kompanie 2112, was equipped with ten Sturmgeschütz III assault guns (2). The first battalion of Panzer-Regiment 29, which had been largely destroyed on the Eastern Front in December 1943, was slowly rebuilt to a strength of forty-five Panther tanks and temporarily attached to the brigade from 5 September. This total included nine Panther ausf A models while the remainder, those received from August 1944, were Panther ausf G versions.

On paper this appeared to be a formidable force but, with the exception of Panzer-Regiment 29, the brigade's formation had been rushed and as early as 10 September 1944 the last units had left Grafenwöhr for the front and were being unloaded near Lunéville in eastern France. At the same time the Allies had managed to cut off and encircle 16.Infanterie-Division near Vittel, south of Nancy, threatening to open a large gap in the German defensive line. The officer commanding Armeegruppe G, Generaloberst Blaskowitz, ordered that

Notes

1. Panzer-Abteilung 115 was the tank battalion of 15.Panzergrenadier-Division.

2. As mentioned earlier the tank destroyer companies were sometimes referred to as the 4.Komapnie of the brigade's Panzer battalion. The companies, with just ten assault guns each, probably relied on the battalion's supply services but were controlled by the brigade headquarters.

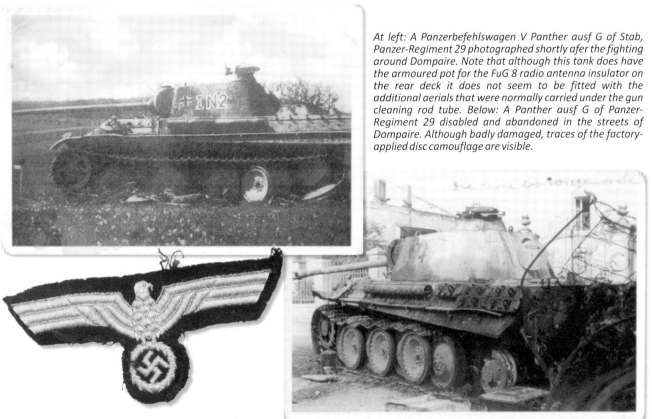

At left: A Panzerbefehlswagen V Panther ausf G of Stab, Panzer-Regiment 29 photographed shortly afer the fighting around Dompaire. Note that although this tank does have the armoured pot for the FuG 8 radio antenna insulator on the rear deck it does not seem to be fitted with the additional aerials that were normally carried under the gun cleaning rod tube. Below: A Panther ausf G of Panzer-Regiment 29 disabled and abandoned in the streets of Dompaire. Although badly damaged, traces of the factory-applied disc camouflage are visible.

A Panther ausf G of 3.Kompanie, Panzer-Regiment 29 photographed at some time after it was captured by units of the French 2nd Armoured Division in Dompaire. The company number 332 is just visible on the turret side depicted in large dark-coloured numbers outlined in white. This tank is also shown on page 25 of the Camouflage & Markings section of this book.

Notes

1. It is difficult to accept the excuse of inexperience coupled with poor weather to explain the neglect of such basic principles and there is some evidence to suggest that the German commanders wilfully underestimated their French opponents.

2. Additionally, in an astounding lapse of discipline, the infantrymen stopped to loot a local garage of a large supply of alcohol.

the front line be restored immediately and Panzer-Brigade 112, with parts of 21.Panzer-Division, were directed to relieve 16.Infanterie-Division and drive back the French 2nd Armoured Division which had in the meantime captured Vittel. Oberst von Usedom divided his brigade into two columns with one containing the Panthers of Panzer-Regiment 29 while the other column was built around the Pzkpfw IV tanks of Panzer-Abteilung 2112. Both columns were supported by a battalion from the brigade's Panzergrenadier-Regiment 2112.

On 12 September 1944 the columns moved off from Épinal and that night the Panthers occupied the village of Dompaire and the neighbouring hamlets of Madonne and Lamerey, about 15 kilometres from their final objective at Vittel. The Pzkpfw IV tanks halted near Darney, almost 20 kilometres to the south-west, and apart from a short engagement fought during the hours of darkness, where the Panther battalion lost one tank, neither column made contact with the enemy. Surprisingly the German units made no attempt to reconnoitre the area around their positions and this would prove decisive in the coming action, particularly at Dompaire (1). Heavy rain fell throughout the night and the French armoured units used this as cover to move into blocking positions to the east and south of the village.

Just after sunrise the Panthers began moving forward along the southern edge of Lamerey and immediately ran into two concealed tank destroyers backed up by strong artillery support. Shortly after this the German positions were pounded by a fighter-bomber assault which the French commander had organised the previous

evening and under cover of the air attack the French tanks moved into Dompaire from the south and also swung behind the Panthers, which were now hemmed in on three sides. At about 11.00 am the fighter bombers returned and this time the skies were completely clear. The effect on Panzer-Regiment 29 was devastating and villagers later reported that German tank crews were seen abandoning their tanks and stealing civilian clothes in an effort to escape. The commander in Dompaire called for help and the Pzkpfw IV tanks of Panzer-Abteilung 2112 with parts of the Panzergrenadier battalion moved towards their comrades and would probably have overrun the French command post at Ville-sur-Ilion, about 3 kilometres south of Dompaire, had not the local civilians warned the French commander (2).

By late afternoon the French had set up a roadblock south of Ville-sur-Ilion consisting of a few tanks and tank destroyers and waiting until the Germans were within 300 metres, opened fire, eventually destroying seven Panzers. The Panzergrenadiers that had been delayed by their drinking bout arrived some time later but were beaten off by two jeeps armed with machine guns. The Panther battalion in Dompaire attempted to break out but was harassed by continuous artillery fire and another air strike and by the end of the day had been reduced to eleven tanks of which only four were in running order. On 14 September 1944 Panzer-Abteilung 2112 reported that just seventeen Pzkpfw IV tanks were serviceable and the two battle groups had suffered over 1,300 casualties. On 23 September 1944 Panzer-Brigade 112 was formally disbanded and the surviving elements, including ten Panthers and twenty-five Pzkpfw IV tanks were absorbed by 21.Panzer-Division.

Panzer-Brigade 113. The formation of this unit began on 2 September 1944 at the Wildflecken and Grafenwöhr training facilities in Germany and like the other third generation brigades it was raised under the Valkyrie mobilisation. The brigade was commanded by Oberst Erich Freiherr von Seckendorf who had served as an cavalry Leutnant in the First World War.

Within a few days the brigade was at full strength, with Panzer-Abteilung 2113 reporting that forty-five Pzkpfw IV tanks were on hand with the staff and three Panzer companies and ten Sturmgeschütz III assault guns with Sturmgeschütz-Kompanie 2113. The first battalion of Panzer-Lehr-Regiment 130, which had only been raised as a Panther battalion in early August 1944 and had recently completed its training, was temporarily subordinated to Panzer-Brigade 113 (1).

Travelling by train to Sarrebourg via Colmar, the brigade was continually harassed by Allied fighter-bombers and by 13 September reported the staggering loss of 230 vehicles. Arriving at the front, Seckendorf was ordered that his brigade should be made ready for combat and he divided his force into two groups. The first, Kampfgruppe Brose, was made up of the first battalion of the Panzergrenadier-Regiment and the Panthers of Panzer-Lehr-Regiment 130 while the second, Kampfgruppe Feiss, contained the Panzergrenadier regiment's second battalion and the Pzkpfw IV tanks. Both groups were supported by Pionier and towed anti-aircraft platoons. On 18 September 1944 the tanks of Panzer-Brigade 113 went into action for the first time near Lunéville and on the following day took part in an attack with 15.Panzergrenadier-Division between the towns of Bezange-la-Petite and Lezey, about 30 kilometres east of Nancy, where thirty of the brigade's tanks were destroyed. On 20 September the brigade reported that just ten Panthers and three Pzkpfw IV tanks were available for deployment and the subsequent actions would be for the most part undertaken by the Panzergrenadiers.

On 22 September 1944 the brigade took part in a last-ditch assault to take the American positions around Arracourt and in two days of fighting was almost completely destroyed, losing its commander, Oberst Seckendorff, who was killed on the last day of the attack (2). On 1 October 1944 the brigade was disbanded with much of the surviving personnel and equipment going to 15.Panzergrenadier-Division. The few remaining Pzkpfw IV tanks of Panzer-Abteilung 2113 were handed over to Panzer-Abteilung 115 and in December the crews were eventually used to form the second battalion of Panzer-Regiment 10. The Panther battalion was withdrawn and returned to its parent formation, Panzer-Lehr-Division, which was at that time refitting in Hungary.

Notes

1. The battalion had been rebuilt from 15 August and had been allocated forty-five Panthers with the last tank arriving on 6 September 1944, the day the brigade began moving to the front.

2. Oberst Seckendorff was posthumously promoted to the rank of Generalmajor on 1 October 1944. He was replaced as commander of Panzer-Brigade 113 by Oberst Arnold Burmeister.

At left: Although this image is of poor quality it is interesting in that it shows what is probably the only Panther tank operated by Panzer-Abteilung 2113. The 500 series of numbers is known to have been used by the battalion staff and the armoured pot on the rear deck identifies this vehicle as a Befehlspanzerwagen. Below: This Panther ausf G of 2.Kompanie, Panzer-Regiment 130 was disabled in late September near Rechicourt, north-east of Metz, when the regiment's first battalion was attached to Panzer-Brigade 113. At that time the brigade formed part of Kampfgruppe Hammon, a battle group made up of the surviving infantry of the first and second battalions of Panzergrenadier-Regiment 2113 and as many as twenty-five tanks, in support of 11.Panzer-Division. The pattern of Zimmerit is typical of vehicles manufactured by the firm of Maschinenfabrik Niedersachsen-Hannover (MAN). This tank is also depicted in the Camouflage & Markings section on page 26.

Notes

1. I have been unable to find an official record of any tanks being allocated at this time although it is possible that the eight Panthers mentioned as being shipped on 2 September 1944 may have had some connection.

2. This was another combat unit formed around parts of Hitler's bodyguard. It was eventually upgraded to brigade and then division status although the latter reorganisation was correct in name only.

Führer-Grenadier Brigade. Officially formed on 10 July 1944 as Kampfgruppe Führer-Grenadier-Brigade under the command of Oberstleutnant Hans-Joachim Kahler, this formation was made up from elements of Ersatz-Brigade Grossdeutschland and men of the Führer-Grenadier-Battalion, a unit of Hitler's bodyguard. The brigade underwent a number of organisational changes during its brief history, some rather confusing, and the tank component originally consisted of a single company (1).

From 2 August 1944 the Führer-Grenadier-Brigade was reorganised with the tank component increased to a full Panzer Abteilung which constituted the brigade's V.Bataillon, sometimes referred to as the Führer-Panzer-Abteilung. The Kampfgruppe was transferred to East Prussia in mid-August 1944 and completed its operational training there subordinated to 4.Armee which was at that time defending the area along the Lithuanian border. In early September 1944, the first battalion, made up of four infantry companies, and the Panzer company were detached and sent to Fallingbostel in Germany and used to form the Führer-Begleit-Regiment (2).

From 14 September 1944 the Führer-Grenadier-Brigade was rebuilt at Cottbus in Germany and the tank component was renamed III.Abteilung and contained four Panzer companies supported by two companies of self-propelled infantry guns and one flamethrower company. It should be noted that this was probably a proposed establishment as the infantry guns are later reported as being controlled directly by the brigade headquarters. I have been unable to find any further mention of the flamethrowers and it is likely that these weapons would have been allocated to the brigade's Pionier-Kompanie.

The reforming of the brigade was apparently a slow process and some elements of the original Kampfgruppe were still fighting in East Prussia around Goldap and Gumbinnen during the last week of October 1944. In early November 1944, III.Abteilung was made up of three companies of Panther tanks, containing a total of nineteen tanks, and a company of Pz IV/70(V) tank destroyers with an additional company of Sturmgeschütz III

Photographed during the Ardennes Offensive, this early production Panther ausf G has been associated with several units but the presence of the Sternantenna D for the FuG 8 command radio, just visible to the left of the turret, and the presence of the hull machine gun may identify this tank as one of the field-modified command Panthers of the Führer-Grenadier-Brigade. Another feature common to this unit were the lengths of spare track completely covering the turret sides.

Photographed outside the Café du Rocher de Felize in the town of Malmedy this vehicle is typical of the converted Panther ausf G tanks of Panzer-Brigade 150. Note the large opening at the turret rear which reveales that the sides are merely sheets of thin metal. The rectangular hole cut into the false front plate allowed the hull machine gun to be used normally. Commanded by Leutnant Gerstenschlager, who was killed in the early stages of the attack, the tank was disabled by accident when the barrel became embedded in the wall of the Café.

assault guns. It is likely that the formation of the Panther battalion was not completed until a few weeks before the commencement of Operation Wacht am Rhein as the last allocation of Panthers was shipped from the Heereszeugamt on 9 December 1944, bringing the total to thirty-six (1).

At some time in that same month the brigade was again reorganised and III.Abteilung was renamed Panzer-Regiment Führer-Grenadier-Brigade although no new tanks were received until 18 February 1945. This renaming process may have been in anticipation of the brigade's expansion to divisional status. The brigade took part in the Ardennes Offensive from 22 December 1944 and was involved in the fighting around Bastogne and the battles for the city of Luxembourg where the commander, Oberstleutnant Kahler, was seriously wounded. On 16 January 1945, with the offensive halted, the brigade was withdrawn from the front line and reformed as the Führer-Grenadier-Division while the tank battalion was renamed Panzer-Regiment 101. The division served on the Eastern Front until the end of the war.

Panzer-Brigade 150. Commanded by Obersturmbannführer Otto Skorzeny, this formation was specifically formed to take part in Unternehmen Greif, the deception operation planned for the Ardennes Offensive. The original plan called for elements of the brigade, disguised as American soldiers, to capture the bridges across the Meuse at Amay, Andenne and Huy. Under the codename Rabenhügel the brigade was organised into three Kampfgruppen referred to as X,Y and Z and although each was supposed to have been outfitted with captured US Army vehicles and equipment only a small number of armoured cars, halftracks and

lorries were available when the offensive began. Indeed many of the uniform items were outdated and the few men who spoke fluent English were grouped into a company-sized formation under Hauptsturmführer Stielau which also contained most of the functioning American equipment. Two M4 Sherman tanks, which were to make up the vanguard, were discarded due to mechanical difficulties and a number of Sturmgeschütz III assault guns and Panther tanks were disguised, rather unconvincingly, as American tank destroyers (2).

The tanks were all Panther ausf G versions shipped directly to the brigade from the Heereszeugamt and the conversion work was carried out at Truppenübungsplatz Grafenwöhr in November and December 1944.

There were minor differences between each vehicle but in general the distinctive cupola was removed and replaced with a simple hatch and sheet metal panels were added to resemble the M10 silhouette. The tanks were repainted, presumably in RAL 6003 Olivegrün or another green shade, and given fake US Army bumper codes which began in XY to identify them to the German military police (3). In the event, they were all used in a conventional assault against the positions of the US 30th Infantry Division along the Malmedy to Spa road and either destroyed in the attack or abandoned after the battle. The brigade was withdrawn from the front on 28 December 1944 but at least one official document mentions a Kampfgruppe Panzer-Brigade 150 in action during the early months of 1945 as under the command of Hauptmann Walter Scherf. An example of one of the brigade's disguised Panthers is shown in the Model Showcase section of this book.

Notes

1. Although thirty-six is the number reported on hand in mid-December it does not take account of the eight tanks mentioned as being allocated on 2 September 1944.

2. The Panthers were attached to Obersturmbannführer Willi Hardieck's Kampfgruppe X. Hardieck was killed when his jeep, ironically one of the few genuine American vehicles on hand, was destroyed by a mine.

3. Although most sources agree that a total of five disguised Pzkpfw V tanks were on hand with Kampfgruppe X some accounts, based on the location of the wrecks, have suggested that as many as ten Panthers were converted.

Throughout its production life the Pzkpfw V Panther was subject to several major redesigns and a series of modifications. These changes were introduced in an effort to increase the tank's performance in combat and to remedy a number of technical problems, many of which bedevilled the design throughout its existence, while others were simply introduced as economy measures. Although the most common variant in service with the independent Panzer brigades was the Panther ausf G, photographic evidence shows that earlier versions were used to some extent and I have included the modifications incorporated into the production of the Panther ausf A model. Further details on the earlier production versions are listed in *Panther Tanks: German Army and Waffen-SS Normandy Campaign 1944*, the third book in this series.

As the earliest allocation was made on 13 July 1944 to Panzer-Brigade 101 and the last known shipment was dispatched to Panzer-Brigade 109 on 7 September, arriving eleven days later, it is reasonable to assume that the Panther ausf G tanks operated by the thirteen brigades were coated in Zimmerit anti-magnetic mine paste and assembled at some time between April and August 1944. The various patterns and methods of application employed by the manufacturers are explained on page 62. The two Panthers allocated to the staff of Panzer-Brigade 103 in January 1945 need not concern us here as the brigade's tank battalion had long been broken up and in any case there is no record of their actual delivery. The tanks of Panzer-Brigade 106, which were incorporated into Panzer-Division Clausewitz in 1945, are examined in the eighteenth book in this series *Panther Tanks: Germany Army and Waffen-SS Defence of the West, 1945.*

The Panther ausf A models known to have been on hand with Panzer-Brigade 102 in Germany and Lithuania would also have received a coat of Zimmerit during production. On 1 August 1944, Panzer-Brigade 103 was allocated three tanks which could possibly have been older models as there is some evidence that they were handed over from one of the Waffen-SS units or the Panzer-Lehr Division after the battles in Normandy.

Panther ausf A was manufactured by the firms of Maschinenfabrik Augsburg-Nürnberg AG (MAN), Daimler-Benz, Maschinenfabrik Niedersachsen Hanover (MNH) and Deutsche Maschinenbau-Aktiengesellschaft (Demag) with production beginning in August 1943 and ending in July 1944. Given that timeframe most of these tanks would have left the assembly plants with a coating of Zimmerit. When the Panther II project was postponed, and eventually abandoned, many of its simplified design aspects were incorporated into the chassis of the Panther ausf G and production began in March 1944. As mentioned above, this version was the most common model in service with the Panzer brigades. All the commercial firms mentioned above were involved in the manufacture of the Panther ausf G except Demag which switched to production of the Bergepanther recovery tank.

Listed below are the major modifications that were incorporated from commencement of the Panther ausf A production run. It should be noted that many of these features were retro-fitted to vehicles returned to Germany for major repairs.

August 1943. The first Panther ausf A models leave the assembly plants. In the same month, operational units were ordered to replace the 16-bolt road wheels with the newer 24-bolt versions.

September 1943. The manufacturers were ordered to apply a coat of Zimmerit anti-magnetic mine paste to all vehicles as part of the assembly process. The exact date that this order was put into effect is unknown and photographs exist of vehicles completed at the beginning of October that do not have Zimmerit, suggesting that some firms at least may have had difficulty obtaining sufficient quantities of the paste. Production of the Panther ausf D ends.

November 1943. A ball mount for the hull machine gun, the Kugelblende, was incorporated into production. As the new mount contained a sight for the machine gun it was felt that the radio operator's forward-facing periscope was now superfluous and it was no longer fitted. The binocular T.Z.F.12 gun sight was replaced by the monocular T.Z.F.12a version. Until supplies of single-aperture gun mantlets were available the second,

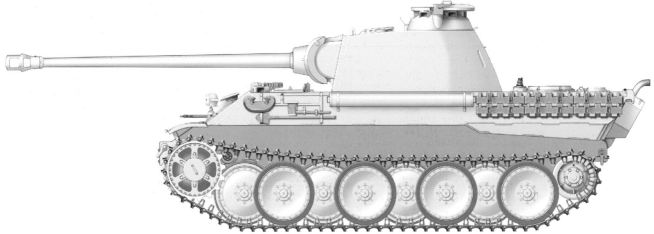

Above: Pzkpfw V Panther ausf A produced after January when the turret side pistol ports were dropped from production. This tank is fitted with the 24-bolt road wheels introduced from August 1943. Note the squared-off joints of the turret sides and the hull front plate. All drawings here are shown without Zimmerit for the sake of clarity.

Above: This Panther ausf A was one of several tanks abandoned in the Jardin du Senat in Paris in August 1944 when the Germans evacuated the city. Manufactured at some time after November 1943, this tank features the cast commander's cupola (A), the aperture for the coaxial machine gun (B), the monocular T.Z.F.12a gun sight (C), the Kugelblende ball mount for the hull machine gun with its plug in place (D), the driver's visor in the open position (E), the single Bosch headlight (F) and the Kgs 64/660/150 tracks with six chevron-shaped cleats. The pattern produced by the application of Zimmerit is indicative of Panthers produced by Daimler-Benz. The suggestion that this was one of four Panthers of Panzer-Regiment 29, Panzer-Brigade 112 captured intact after the fighting around Dompaire, although widely accepted, is incorrect. This tank is today on display in the grounds of the barracks of the French Army's 501-503ème Régiment de Chars de Combat at Mourmelon-le-Grand outside the city of Reims.

outer sight aperture was sealed with an armoured plug although these vehicles retained the wider rain channel. A number of tanks produced in November and December 1943 were fitted with a towing coupling bolted onto the hull rear plate along the lower edge below the engine access hatch. This was identical to the coupling fitted to the Bergepanther recovery vehicle (1). Units in the field were ordered to apply Zimmerit to those tanks which had not received a coat before leaving the factories.

December 1943. The small pistol ports, referred to as MP Stopfen, on either side of the turret were dropped from production. It was intended that these be replaced by the Nahverteidigungswaffe, or close defence weapon, which was to be mounted in the turret roof, could be traversed through 360 degrees and was capable of firing smoke candles, grenades and flares. A hole was cut in the turret roof, to the right of the cupola, into which the Nahverteidigungswaffe was meant to be fitted but due to difficulties with supply none were available until March 1944 and the turrets of many Panther ausf A models assembled in February and March were instead fitted with a circular plate covering the hole and held in place by four bolts.

January 1944. Two cooling pipes were added to the engine exhaust manifold on the left-hand side.

February 1944. A vertical mount for the 20-ton jack replaced the previous horizontal arrangement which held a 15-ton jack. Beginning in February, a towing coupling was welded to the engine access hatch on the hull rear plate although MNH Panthers were assembled until mid-April with the old access hatch.

Notes

1. As this interfered with ground clearance it was soon dropped from production and although the number of tanks actually fitted with the coupling was small, most Panther ausf A models manufactured up to April 1944 had the necessary brackets and holes, the latter sealed with four bolts.

Above: Pzkpfw V Panther ausf G produced in late March or early April 1944. The most distinctive feature of the Panther ausf G was the angled sides of the redesigned hull, fabricated from single plates. The turret was initially the same as the Panther ausf A with its cast cupola and only differed in small details as production continued. Other new features included the driver's and radio-operator's hatches, which were now hinged as opposed to the pivoting versions, and the deletion of the prominent driver's visor. In place of the latter a periscope with an armoured cover was installed on the hull roof in front of the driver's hatch. The single Bosch headlight was moved from the glacis to the left fender. The hull Schürzen, or armoured skirts, were now fixed to an extended track guard which was fixed to the hull sides. In addition, the tool stowage on the hull sides was revised. The rear deck was completely redesigned including the louvres and the air intakes.

Notes

1. These last two modifications were also to be carried out by units in the field and incorporated into the assembly of the Panther ausf A, which was still in production.

2. These patterns and the colours used are discribed in some detail in *Panther Tanks: Germany Army and Waffen-SS Defence of the West, 1945.*

3. This was first put into effect at MNH two days later when Panther Fahrgestellnummer 128562 left the assembly line.

March 1944. The first production models of the Panther ausf G were completed. In fact, just two tanks were completed in March and large-scale production did not really begin until the following month when MAN assembled 105 vehicles.

May 1944. To simplify construction, the cast armoured guards that protected the exhaust pipes where they entered the hull were replaced by welded versions.

June 1944. Sheet metal covers were fitted over the exhaust pipes above the armoured guards. These pipes regularly become hot enough to produce a visible glow, making the tank an easy target. In response to complaints from tank crews that the turret rear access hatch could not be opened from the outside, a handle was added. Three sockets, or Pilzen, were welded to the turret roof to accommodate the 2-ton Befehlskran jib boom (1).

July 1944. It was found that the periscopes fitted to the commander's cupola were liable to come loose if the tank experienced any violent vibration and, in addition, they were difficult to remove and replace. In this month, a frame and improved fastener were installed. At the same time the assembly plants were ordered to cease the installation of a mount for an observation periscope, or Sehstab, in the cupola. Both these modifications were essentially internal and are rarely seen in photographs. On 17 July, the decision was taken to drop the air intake cover on the front hull from production but this was reversed within days. Production of the Panther ausf A was wound up with MNH producing the last eleven tanks to leave the assembly lines.

August 1944. In line with an order issued in the previous month, a rain guard was fitted over the driver's periscope. A metal debris guard was added to the turret roof to cover the gap behind the mantlet of the main gun. The hatches of the driver and radio operator were fitted with new hinge fasteners which allowed the hatches to be opened upward and jettisoned in an emergency. From mid-August, camouflage patterns were applied at the assembly plants. The familiar base colour of Dunkelgelb RAL 7028 was retained, over which large patches of Olivgrün RAL 6003 and Rotbraun RAL 8017 were painted, covering approximately two-thirds of the surface area. The relevant order stressed that every effort was to be made to deliver the remaining August consignment in the new factory-applied schemes and as a total of 356 vehicles were assembled in that month, perhaps as many as one-third of that number received the new camouflage. It was during this period that tanks were painted in the so-called ambush and disc camouflage schemes. A number of Panther ausf G tanks were painted in one of these factory-applied schemes before the application of Zimmerit was dropped from the production process and examples of these are shown in the Camouflage & Markings section (2).

September 1944. On 7 September 1944, the Generalinspekteur der Panzertruppen ordered the end of the application of Zimmerit anti-magnetic mine paste (3). Interior surfaces were no longer to be painted with Elfenbein RAL 1001 but instead left in their primer coat. A new gun mantlet, which featured a prominent chin, or Kinnblende, was incorporated into production. Its introduction was, however, slow and the earlier round design was used until the end of the war. A lengthened rain guard was fitted over the sight aperture of the gun mantlet. A small number of vehicles were fitted with FG 1250 infrared searchlights and sighting equipment. A limited number of MAN produced vehicles, perhaps as few as twenty-four, were fitted with steel-tyred roadwheels.

Above: A Panther ausf G of 2.Kompanie, Panzer-Abteilung 2107 disabled and abandoned on 13 October 1944 near Overloon in the Netherlands. This tank, Fahrgestellnummer 128427, was assembled by MNH in July 1944 and delivered to Panzer-Brigade 107 in the following month. Note the welded exhaust guards, fitted to these tanks from May 1944, and the sheet metal covers introduced in the following month. The pattern of Zimmerit, made up of horizontal strokes, is indicative of MNH-produced Panthers and has also been applied, in a reverse fashion, behind the wheels. The track guard which normally held the hull Schürzen and the rear stowage boxes were easily damaged as can be seen here. Another photograph of this tank can be seen on page 2 and it is also depicted in the Camouflage & Markings section of this book. Below: This Panther ausf G of Panzer-Abteilung 2107 was also abandoned during the fighting around Overloon and restored to running order by its British captors. Interestingly, other images of this tank show that it was fitted with one of the ribbed rear stowage boxes mounted on some MNH-produced Panther tanks and Jagdpanther tank destroyers from September 1944 (inset).

Notes

1. Neither the Western Allies nor the Soviets produced magnetic mines of their own design but there are instances of captured weapons being used against German tanks during the battles in Russia in 1943.

2. The company had marketed a number of products under the Zimmerit name and it is possible that the paste used from 1943 was a refinement of an existing commodity.

3. As a matter of interest, the firm of Henschel, which assembled the Tiger, is known to have experimented with a similar product well before the general introduction of Zimmerit.

A prominent feature of German tanks and assault guns of this period was Zimmerit. This will be familiar to many readers as a thick paste applied to the surfaces of armoured vehicles before they left the assembly plants which was intended to neutralise magnetic mines.

From 1942, German infantry units were issued with a series of anti-tank grenades, collectively referred to as Hafthohlladung, which could be held to a metal surface by small but powerful magnets. When the component charge was detonated the resulting explosion was sufficient to penetrate up to 140mm of armour plate or destroy a tank's tracks, effectively disabling the vehicle. Assuming that their enemies would very quickly develop a similar weapon, the Germans began to look for a countermeasure and it was decided that altering the flat, smooth surfaces of their own tanks would protect them from the enemies grenades (1).

To achieve this, a putty or thick paste was to be applied to all the vertical and sloped surfaces of tanks and assault guns, including the hull sides behind the wheels, to the height that an average man could reach before the vehicles left the assembly plants. Moving parts and detachable items, such as hinges and tools, were not to be coated as it was expected that the paste would be quickly worn away. Officially, the paste was not to be applied to either hull or turret Schürzen although photographic evidence shows that this order was frequently ignored. The firm of Chemische Werke Zimmer & Co. of Berlin, which specialised in sealants and adhesives, was contracted to supply large quantities of a thick paste referred to as Zimmerit (2). The use of Zimmerit was explained in some detail in the third book in this series *Panther Tanks: German Army and Waffen-SS Normandy Campaign 1944*, but it may be helpful to repeat some of that information here. The application of the paste was quite complicated and required two coats, with each coat needing at least four hours to cure. Once dry, the paste became quite hard and it was then softened with a blowtorch and, with special tools, fashioned into a pattern of ridges or grids which can, in most cases, identify the manufacturer of a particular tank. It should be stressed that it was these ridges or grids which denied the magnets the flat surface they required and the paste itself had no inherent anti-magnetic properties.

In mid-1945, after Germany's surrender, the British Army conducted an extensive investigation into the use and application of Zimmerit and a chemical analysis showed that the paste was composed mainly of Barium Sulphate and Polyvinyl Acetate, which most readers will be familiar with as white PVA glue, with the addition of an ochre pigment and Zinc Sulphide. The reaction of Barium Sulphate with Zinc Sulphide tends to produce a white colour which would have lightened the ochre pigment somewhat. As a binding agent, ordinary sawdust was added. Apparently the paste as delivered had a very strong, unpleasant smell of acetone, but was easy to handle and to apply to the surface of the vehicle, requiring no preparation of the bare metal plates, although tanks were painted with an anti-corrosive primer as a matter of course.

The application of Zimmerit was instituted in September 1943, although the exact date is not known and may have differed from one assembly plant to another (3).

Above: Examples of Zimmerit applied to Panther tanks. A. MAN Panther ausf A. Note the absence of the vertical grid line. B. MAN Panther ausf A. The more commonly seen pattern. C. MNH Panther ausf A. D. MNH Panther auf G. E. Daimler-Benz Panther ausf G. F. The distinctive Demag pattern applied to a Panther ausf A.

The production of the Panther ausf D model was halted in the same month that saw the introduction of Zimmerit and as just thirty-seven of these tanks left the assembly lines before production was halted in September, it is unlikely that many received a coat at the factories (1). As the great majority of Panther ausf A tanks were manufactured between September 1943 and July 1944 it is likely that almost all would have been coated with Zimmerit during the assembly phase. Production of the Panther ausf G began in March 1944, with the first tanks reaching front-line units in April, meaning that as many as 1,600 vehicles could have been coated in Zimmerit before 9 September 1944 when the practice ceased. Most of the tanks allocated to the independent Panzer brigades fall into this last category.

Each company created special tools to complete the application of Zimmerit and, as mentioned earlier, the resulting pattern of ridges or grids which can identify the manufacturer of a particular tank. It should mentioned that these conclusions have been arrived at largely by the examination of photographic evidence and should best be regarded as a general rule to which possible exceptions exist.

MAN Panther ausf A. The Zimmerit coating was typically made up of short vertical strokes applied with a roller which gave a very orderly and consistent appearance. Over the short strokes or ridges, vertical and horizontal lines forming a grid of about 10 centimetres square were worked into the paste with a pallet knife or trowel. These longer lines were less orderly and could sometimes be applied diagonally, particularly on mudguards and stowage bins but also on the turret sides.

MAN Panther ausf G. The pattern that had been applied to the Panther ausf A models was maintained but in a more uniform manner with different vehicles displaying the same number of lines on turret sides, hull fronts and other surfaces. Diagonal lines are rarely seen. Another similar pattern was used, employing a slightly larger roller which left a thicker coat of Zimmerit and necessitated a grid of about 15 centimetres square. That this pattern does not seem to have been applied to surfaces such as mudguards may suggest that it was a later version. It seems that Zimmerit was not applied to the commander's cupola on any MAN variants (2).

MNH Panther ausf A. The coating applied to Panther ausf A models featured a flat, rather smooth application broken up by deeply scored vertical and horizontal lines which formed a grid. As a general rule Zimmerit was not applied to the mudguards and even the stowage bins were left untreated on some vehicles.

Although rare, there are instances of this pattern being extended to the commander's cupola.

MNH Panther ausf G. In July 1944, MNH switched to production of the Panther ausf G and the pattern was changed to one made up of deep horizontal strokes applied with a trowel, often referred to today as the 'ladder pattern'. Over this, an orderly grid of approximately 10 centimetres square was inscribed with a trowel or similar tool. This process could only have been in use for just over nine weeks and photographic examples are quite rare. In addition, it is possible that the very first Panther ausf G tanks assembled by MNH featured the patterns seen on the firm's Panther ausf A vehicles.

Daimler-Benz Panther ausf A. This pattern was characterised by a rather flat application which was afterwards roughened with short strokes often, but not always, made on the diagonal. The surface was then broken up by vertical and horizontal lines which formed a grid which could also be very roughly applied, the lines often straying off course. The grid also varied considerably in size but did not extend to the cupola. With the exception of the initial rough application, this pattern can be very similar to that seen on Panther tanks produced by MNH and the two are often difficult, if not impossible, to differentiate in photographs.

Daimler-Benz Panther ausf G. The pattern used on the earlier version was maintained with the grid varying in size from quite large, as seen on the MNH Panther ausf G models, to the so-called 'small square' version applied to the Jagdpanthers built by MIAG. However, a grid of approximately 10 centimetre squares is most commonly seen in photographs. There is some evidence that Daimler-Benz adopted this pattern, identified by its roughened finish, solely to distinguish their Panthers from those produced by the company's main rival, MAN.

Demag Panther ausf A. This pattern was made up of short horizontal strokes, probably applied with a trowel, which were then separated by deep vertical lines. Some vehicles also featured horizontal lines which then formed a grid and this has led to the Demag patterns being incorrectly assumed to be a version of the MAN Zimmerit.

Many photographs exist of tanks coated in patterns which do not conform to the styles mentioned above but these are usually earlier models, most notably the Panther ausf D, and very few would have been used by the units covered by this book. These patterns are usually characterised by a rough surface, suggesting a hurried application, and may have been applied by units in the field as directed from November 1943.

Notes

1. Most photographs of Panther ausf D variants coated with Zimmerit, serving in both the East and in France during 1944, seem to indicate that the paste was not applied in any consistent manner but rather in a rough and hurried fashion.

2. Interestingly, it has been suggested that the grid was applied to the first coat of Zimmerit while the vertical strokes were worked into the second although this could not be possible with a diagonal grid.

Dragon Models Ltd
B1-10/F., 603-609 Castle Peak Rd,
Kong Nam Industrial Building,
Tsuen Wan, N. T., Hong Kong
www.dragon-models.com

Tamiya Inc
Shizuoka City, Japan
www.tamiya.com

Trumpeter/Hobby Boss
NanLong Industrial Park,SanXiang,
ZhongShan,GuangDong, China
www.trumpeter-china.com
www.hobbyboss.com

Academy Plastic Models
521-1, Yonghyeon-dong, Uijeongbu-si,
Gyeonggi-do, Korea
www.academy.co.kr

Hobby Fan/ AFV Club
6F ., No.183, Sec. 1, Datong Rd, Xizhi City,
Taipei County 221, Taiwan
www.hobbyfan.com

Royal Model
Via E. Montale, 19-95030 Pedara, Italy
www.royalmodel.com

Italeri S.p.A.
via Pradazzo 6/b,
40012 Calderara di Reno, Bologna, Italy
www.italeri.com

Takom
www.takom-world.com

Meng-Model
Galaxy Century Bldg., No. 3069 Caitian Rd.,
Futian Dist., Shenzhen, Guangdong, China
www.meng-model.com

Amusing Hobby
3-16-19 Ima, Kita-ku, Okayama, Japan
www.amusinghobby.com

Rye Field Models
www.ryefield-model.com
An almost non-existent website. I would
recommend one of the on-line retailers.

Hauler
Jan Sobotka,
Moravská 38, 620 00 Brno,
Czech Republic
www.hauler.cz

Voyager
Room 501, No.411 4th Village,
SPC Jinshan District, Shanghai 200540
P.R.China
www.voyagermodel.com

Griffon Model
Suite 501, Bldg 01, 418 Middle Longpan Rd,
Nanjing, China
www.griffonmodel.com

Aber
ul. Jalowcowa 15, 40-750 Katowice, Poland
www.aber.net.pl

E.T. Model
www.etmodeller.com

Friulmodel
H 8142. Urhida, Nefelejcs u. 2., Hungary
www.friulmodel.hu

Modelkasten
Chiyoda-ku Kanda, Nishiki-Cho 1-7, Tokyo,
Japan
www.modelkasten.com
Very difficult to navigate but worthwhile.

Airfix
www.airfix.com

Revell
www.revell.com

Eduard Model Accessories
Mirova 170, 435 21 Obrnice,
Czech Republic
www.eduard.com

Master Club
www.masterclub.ru
It appears that this firm is closely associated
with Armour35, a Russsian mail-order firm.

Model Artisan Mori
Yasutsugu Mori,
Maison Suiryu 302, Kunoshiro-cho 1-10,
Yokkaichi-City, Mie 510-0072, Japan
www.artisanmori.web.fc2.com

Model Factory Hiro
Yubinbango 121-0063 Adachi-ku, Tokyo,
Higashihokima 2-Chome, 3-8 Japan
www.modelfactoryhiro.com

RB Model
Powstancow Wlkp.29B,
64-360 Zbaszyn,
Poland
www.rbmodel.com

M Workshop Singapore
91 Bencoolen St, Sunshine Plaza 01-58,
Singapore
www.themworkshop.com

Zvezda (Zvezda-America)
www.zvezda-usa.com
Note that the Russian catalogue is not the
same as the US version.

ROCHM Model
www.rochmmodel.com
rochmmodel@gmail.com
This company has a huge selection of parts
and accessories for 1/35 scale Panther
models.

In writing this book I referred extensively to *Germany's Panther, The Quest for Combat Supremacy* written by the late Thomas L. Jentz with plan drawings by Hilary L. Doyle. Another invaluable resource are Thomas Jentz's *Panzertruppen* books which I would recommend to any reader with an interest in German armour. I should also acknowledge the contributors to Brett Green's Missing Lynx discussion forum, particularly Ron Owen Hayes who has spent years studying the independent Panzer brigades. I also relied heavily on the work of Martin Block and the late Ron Klages whose research on unit histories and vehicle allocations would fill many volumes. I would like to thank the modellers who graciously allowed me to publish the images of their work and I must make special mention of Roberto Reale of Royal Model, Sheng Hui of ROCHM, Jan Zdiarsky from Eduard Accessories and Freddie Leung of Dragon Models who all helped enormously. As always, I am indebted to Karl Berne, Valeri Polokov and J.Howard Parker for their invaluable assistance with the photographs and period insignia.

A Pzkpfw V Panther ausf G of I.Abteilung, Panzer-Regiment 16 photographed during the fighting around Arracourt in late September 1944. At this time the battalion was attached to Panzer-Brigade 111 and this tank is also shown and discussed on page 24 of the Camouflage & Markings section of this book.